BABIES' NAMES

Louise Nicholson

Illustrated by Ian Beck

Conran Octopus

First published in 1987 by
Conran Octopus Limited
37 Shelton Street
London WC2H 9HN

Reprinted 1989, 1990 (twice), 1991 (twice),
1992 (thrice), 1993, 1994 (twice), 1995, 1996 (twice)

Typeset by Elite Typesetting Techniques
Printed in Hong Kong

ISBN 1 85029 111X

CONTENTS

INTRODUCTION

I love my name. I like its sound, its meaning and its associations. When I was tiny, the local grocer serenaded me with 'Every little breeze Seems to whisper Louise' while I surveyed the sweet counter. As I grew up, it was neither too short nor too long, although there was an inevitable Lulu at school. Now I find Louise is unusual enough for me rarely to be 'which Louise?'. But it is common enough for people I meet to know how to pronounce and spell it. My parents made a perfect choice.

In the following pages there are names to suit the most romantic (Tanya) or ambitious (Nicholas) parent, and many that simply sound beautiful. Choosing a name is fun, but just one word of warning: do check up on how the initials will read. A David Orlando Gibbs will have a tough school life with his pencil case marked 'D.O.G.'

LOUISE NICHOLSON

Abigail: A father's happiness, fount of joy. In the Bible, one of King David's wives was kindly Abigail. Popular with the Puritans, the name was revived in the 1970s. Other forms: Abbey, Gail, Gale, Gayle.

Adelaide: Noble position. The capital of South Australia was named after William IV's wife, Queen Adelaide, in 1836.

Adele: Noble. William the Conqueror's fourth daughter was called Adela, a popular name in France though less common in Britain. Other forms: Adelia, Adelina, Della.

Adeline: Noble. Another Norman introduction boosted last century in the popular song where Sweet Adeline is 'the flower of my heart'. Other forms: Adaline, Adelina, Edelin, Lina.

Agatha: Good woman. St Agatha, the martyr whose veil is believed to have saved Sicily when Mount Etna erupted, is the patron saint of fire protection. A favourite Victorian name, given to Dame Agatha Mary Clarissa Christie (1891–1975), writer of detective novels.

Agnes: Purity, chasteness. Two saints Agnes were martyred for their self-denial and piousness, making the name as popular in Tudor times as Joan and Elizabeth. Now mostly a Scottish choice. Other forms: Aggy, Anis, Annice, Nancy.

Aileen: *See* Eileen.

Alexandra: Defender, protector of mankind. The name has royal associations through Edward VII's wife, who founded Alexandra Rose Day, and Princess Alexandra (Mrs Angus Ogilvy), who was born on Christmas Day 1936 and christened Alexandra Helen Olga Christabel. Other forms: Alex, Alexei, Sacha, Sandra, Zandra.

Alfreda: Intelligent and wise advice. Popular with fashionable Victorians and Edwardians whose medieval heroes included King Alfred the Great (849–99). Other forms: Freda, Freddy.

Alice: Of noble birth. A medieval name made more popular by Lewis Carroll's *Alice in Wonderland* (1865). Queen Victoria chose it for one daughter, and in 1950 the Queen chose it as Princess Anne's third name. Other forms: Alicia, Alise, Alison, Alyce, Elissa, Lycia.

Alison: Son of Alice. A Gaelic form of Alice which, since the 1930s, has spread out of Scotland to become as popular as Alice. Other forms: Alisoun, Allyson.

Allegra: Joyful, lively. An Italian name given to Byron's daughter and, more recently and very aptly, to the American ballet dancer Allegra Kent.

Alma: Generous, warm-hearted. The term 'Alma Mater', meaning foster-mother, was an affectionate nickname coined by the Romans for several of their favourite goddesses.

Althea: Healing, healthy. An unusual Greek name which is also the botanical family name for the hollyhock.

Amabel: Lovable. Popular in medieval Britain, this is now an unusual choice despite its meaning. Other forms: Amabella, Mabel.

Amanda: Deserving of love. A popular name since Noel Coward revived it with his comedy *Private Lives* (1930). Other forms: Manda, Mandi, Mandy.

Amarinda: Unfading, everlasting. A name poets give to an imaginary, ever-flowering, ever-beautiful blossom.

Amber: Deep yellow resin. A resin that is polished to make jewellery and ornaments, it is believed to have powers to cure.

Ambrosia: Food of life, immortality. The name for the food eaten by the mythological gods to perpetuate their immortality was later used for any food or smell fit for the gods.

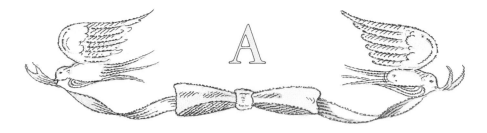

Amelia: Industrious, earnest work. A German name that is also popular in its anglicised form, Emily. Other forms: Amalea, Ameline, Amy, Emelita, Emmeline.

Amorette: Little love, sweetheart. One of several names made up by writers to describe a character, this one was invented by Edmund Spenser in his poem *The Faerie Queene* (1590).

Amy: Loved. From the French name Aimée. Revived last century by Charles Dickens' *Little Dorrit* (1855–7) and by Louisa M. Alcott's *Little Women* (1868–9). The Scottish form is Esme. Other forms: Ana, Nastasya, Stacy, Tasia.

Anastasia: She will rise again. Its meaning has led to this name often being given to an Easter baby. Once associated with the Virgin Mary's apocryphal midwife, it is now used mainly as a Russian import, often as Nastasia or Stacey. Other forms: Ana, Nastaya, Stacy, Tasia.

Andrea: Manly. A very popular Scottish name that is probably derived from Aindrea, the Gaelic form of Andrew. Other forms: Andra, Andria, Andrina, Dreena, Rena.

Angela: Bringer of good tidings. The name is sometimes given to girls born on September 29, the festival of St Michael and All Angels. Other forms: Angel, Angie, Anjela.

Angelica: Angelic. A name implying angel-like perfection.

Angharad: Much beloved. A Welsh name whose anglicised form is Ancret. Other forms: Ancreta, Ingaret.

Anita: Favoured by God, fortunate. The Spanish diminutive of Ann, used in Britain since World War II. Other form: Nita.

Anna: Favoured by God, fortunate. The Greek and Latin forms of Hannah. Consistently popular in Europe for its association with Anna, the apocryphal mother of the Virgin Mary. Later given a boost by Leo Tolstoy's *Anna Karenina* (1875–7) and Dame Anna Neagle (1904–86), the British dancer and actress. Other forms: Ana, Anina, Anita, Annah, Annette, Annice, Nana, Nanette, Nanna.

Annabel: Fortunate and beautiful. In England the name comes from Anna and Bella; in Scotland from Amabel, meaning 'lovable'. Other forms: Anabel, Annabella, Annabelle, Mabel.

Anne: Favoured by God, fortunate. The French form of Hannah, spelt with or without an 'e'. Always a popular name in Britain, it was chosen by the Queen for her daughter Anne Elizabeth Alice

Louise. Other forms: Ann, Annie, Anouska, Nan, Nancy, Nina, Ninette.

Annunciata: Bringer of news. Through its association with the Annunciation – when the angel from God told Mary she would give birth to Christ – this is an apt name for a Christmas baby.

Anthea: Like a flower. With its associations of blossoming beauty and fragrance, this name was often given by poets to the Greek goddess of spring. A popular 1940s name.

Antonia: Flowering, flourishing. Italian female form of Anthony, made popular by several saints. The French form – Antoinette – was the name of the cultured queen, Marie Antoinette, wife of Louis XVI. Other forms: Antonette, Antonica, Tanya, Tonia, Tonya.

Aphrodite: Created from foam or dust. Born out of the sea's waves, Aphrodite, the Greek goddess of love and fertility, was the personification of grace, beauty and charm.

April: Ready for the sun. The use of this month as a first name, with its springtime association of new life, began only this century.

Arabella: Moved by prayer. The medieval Scottish name Orabilis became Orabella, Arbell and Arabella before reaching England, to be promoted by the black-eyed young lady in Charles Dickens' *The Pickwick Papers* (1837).

Ariadne: Most divine. In Greek mythology Ariadne cast her crown to the skies where it was transformed into a group of stars. Other forms: Ariana, Arianna.

Artemisia: Artemis, Greek goddess of the moon, animals and hunting, and lover of music. She swept across the sky by night and roamed the countryside by day. Other forms: Artemesia, Artemisa.

Athena: Athene, Greek goddess of wisdom, civilisation and household skills, armed herself to protect mortal heroes.

Audrey: Noble. A form of the Old English name Ethel. St Etheldreda, known as Audrey, died of a throat tumour and necklaces or 'tawdry' are sold on her feast-day. Its more recent popularity was helped by the actress Audrey Hepburn whose real name is Edda.

Augusta: Venerable. A royal favourite introduced from Germany by the Hanoverians. More recently, the name of Bertie Wooster's formidable aunt in P. G. Wodehouse's stories. Other forms: Augustina, Gusta.

Aurora: Dawn. The beautiful Roman goddess of the dawn mourned her son's death with daily tears, the origin of morning dew. Other forms: Aurore, Ora.

Averil: Boar-like protection. An Old English name with religious overtones because wild boar-heads were offered to pagan gods.

Barbara: Strange, foreign. A name honouring St Barbara whose father killed her and was promptly struck by lightning. She therefore protects against lightning and is also patron of architects, engineers and miners. Its 20th-century revival was helped by Shaw's *Major Barbara* (1907) and by the Hollywood film star Barbara Stanwyck, whose real name was Ruby Stevens. Other forms: Babs, Barbi, Barby, Bobbie.

Bathsheba: Daughter of a vow, of fulfilment. The name of the unscrupulous, but later penitent, mistress of King David and mother of King Solomon was a favourite in medieval Europe. Never fashionable since, despite being given to Thomas Hardy's heroine in *Far From The Madding Crowd*. Other forms: Bathshua, Sheba.

Beatrice: Bringer of happiness. The unattainable Beatrice in Dante's *Divina Commedia* personified spiritual love and was the perfect medieval heroine. Revived last century, when Queen Victoria chose it for her ninth child. Other forms: Beatrix, Beatty, Trixy.

Belinda: Beautiful snake. In ancient Scandinavia, snakes symbolised wisdom and immortality. Gained popularity in Britain when given to the heroine of Alexander Pope's satirical poem *The Rape of the Lock* (1714). Other forms: Belynda, Linda, Lindy.

Belle: Beautiful. A French name whose Italian form is Bella. Other forms: Bel, Bella.

Bernadette: Bear-like bravery. Rose to popularity after Marie Bernadette Soubirous (died 1879), canonised in 1933, was cured by the healing waters at Lourdes. Other forms: Bernadine, Bernadot, Bernetta.

Bertha: Bright. A royal favourite in medieval Europe, through the Emperor Charlemagne's mother, then revived in the 19th century by Victorian medievalists. Other forms: Berta, Bertina.

Beryl: Dazzling pure stone. An ancient word meaning a jewel with the qualities of clarity, preciousness and the power to bring good luck. Popular with the Edwardians, who favoured jewel names.

Beth: Breath of life. A Scottish name from the Gaelic. Also a short form of Elizabeth. Other forms: Beathag, Bethia.

Bethany: Worshipper of God. This Hebrew name – in the Bible it was the village where Lazarus lived – is now gaining popularity. Other form: Bethanie.

Beverley: Beaver's meadow or stream. The fashionable Beverly Hills in Los Angeles, not the Yorkshire town, inspired the name which crossed the Atlantic to become a British favourite in the 1950s.

Bianca: White. An Italian name, implying purity. In Shakespeare's *Taming of the Shrew*, Bianca is the placid sister of Kate,

the 'shrew'. Other forms: Biancha, Blanca, Blanche, Blandina.

Billie: Determined. An Old English name, although today it is mostly used as a female form of William.

Blanche: *See* Bianca.

Blithe: Gentle, mild. In Noel Coward's *Blithe Spirit* (1941), the playful ghost of the hero's first wife materialises to tease her husband and successor.

Bonnie: Good, beautiful. A Scottish name made popular by Margaret Mitchell's *Gone with the Wind* (1936), in which Rhett Butler's daughter is known as Bonnie Blue Butler because of her beautiful blue eyes. The film *Bonnie and Clyde* (1967) kept it in vogue.

Brenda: Sword. Always a popular Scottish name, it eventually spread to England to become a favourite choice in the 1940s.

Bridget: High, exalted. The Celtic goddess of fire, light and poetry, and an Irish saint, made this one of the most popular names in Ireland. Brigitte Bardot popularised the French version. Other forms: Biddie, Birgitta, Brigid, Brit.

Bronwen: White-bosomed. Welsh legends tell of Bronwen, daughter of Wyr, the god of the sea, yet the name has only recently become popular.

Brook: Reward, enjoyment. This Old English word was originally adopted as a name for both sexes. Other form: Brooke.

Bryony: To swell, grow bigger. Despite being the botanical name for a climbing plant with poisonous berries, this was a popular first name during the 1930s, and is coming back into fashion.

Bunty: Little rabbit, bunny. A pet name made famous through the heroine of the stage comedy *Bunty Pulls the Strings* (1911).

Caitlin: Pure. The Irish form of Catherine. As Kathleen, it reached Britain last century.

Camilla: Witness at a ritual. The name of the goddess Diana's noble attendant in Roman mythology, it has been popular since the last century, together with the French form, Camille. Other forms: Cammie, Millie, Milly.

Candida: White hot. A popular Roman name but hardly found in Britain until this century, encouraged by the gentle heroine of Shaw's *Candida* (1898). Other forms: Candice, Candy.

Carly: Free woman, country woman. Long popular in the US, it has now crossed the Atlantic and entered the 1980s' top favourite girls' names. Other forms: Carla, Carley, Carlita, Karla.

Carmen: Garden, paradise. The sensuous gipsy heroine of Bizet's opera *Carmen* (1873–5). Other forms: Carmine, Charmain.

Carol: Celebration in song and dance. Originally a form of Caroline, it is a name for both sexes, and is now associated with Christmas songs. The actress Carole Lombard chose it in favour of her real name, Jane. Other forms: Carey, Carola, Caryl, Karel, Sherry, Sheryl.

Caroline: Woman, housewife. As the Italian female form of Charles, the name came to Britain in the 18th century with George II's bride and was instantly fashionable. Still popular today. Other forms: Carolina, Carolyn, Karolyn, Sharleen, Sharlene.

Casey: Watchful, brave. An Irish name for girls and boys, made famous by the ballads about Casey Jones (1864–1900), the heroic train engineer who saved passengers' lives after the Cannon Ball Express accident.

Cassandra: Confuser of men. Greek myths tell how Apollo gave the beautiful Cassandra powers of prophecy, but when she was unfaithful he made her gift a curse and her prophecies disbelieved. Popular in medieval romances, but it has never really been in fashion.

Catherine: Pure. St Catherine, who was tortured on a spiked wheel (hence the name given to wheel-shaped fireworks), inspired a medieval cult following. Popular in Tudor times – it was the name of three of Henry VIII's wives – it is still a favourite. See also Kate. Other forms: Caitlin, Catharine, Cathrine, Cathy, Catriona, Karen, Karina, Katarina, Katharine, Katrina, Kay, Kerry, Kitty.

Cecilia: Blind. The Italian saint who is patroness of music was martyred for consecrating her virginity to God at her

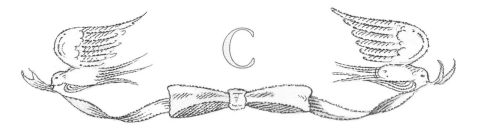

wedding. Introduced to England by William the Conqueror, who named his daughter Cecilia. Other forms: Cicely, Sisley.

Celia: Divine place, heaven. It is to Celia that the poet Ben Jonson wrote the lines 'Drink to me only with thine eyes, And I will pledge with mine'. Other forms: Celeste, Selina, Sheila.

Charlotte: Free woman. This French female form of Charles came to Britain with the Normans but was popularised by George III's queen, Charlotte Sophia, and is a firm favourite today. Other forms: Charleen, Charlie, Charlotta, Cheryl, Lolita, Lottie.

Charmian: Joy. Shakespeare introduced the name to Britain through the queen's attendant in *Antony and Cleopatra*.

Cherry: Small, sweet, red fruit. From the French name, Cerise, although it is also a short form of Charity, one of the Puritan 'virtue' names.

Cheryl: Dear, beloved or sweet cherry. The name first appeared in the 1920s, adapted from the French words 'chère' meaning dear or 'cerise' meaning cherry, and was further anglicised to Sheryl. Other forms: Cheralyn, Cherilynn, Cheryle, Cheryll, Sheral, Sherilyn.

Chloë: Flourishing green shoot. The name for the Greek goddess of young crops has recently become popular. Other forms: Clea, Cloe.

Christine: Anointed. A popular name since medieval times for its associations of blessings and Christian kindness. Other forms: Chrissy, Christina, Karstin, Kirsty, Kristin, Tina.

Cicely: *See* Cecilia.

Claire: Shining brightly. The 12th-century St Clare of Assisi, a follower of St Francis, is now patron saint of television since she is said to have once miraculously watched a mass from a long way away. Other forms: Chiara, Claira, Clara, Clare, Clarice, Clarie.

Claudine: Lame. This French form of Claudius became popular in Britain only in the 1960s. Other forms: Claudette, Claudia.

Colette: The people's triumph. A short form for Nicolette, a French name which came to Britain in the 1940s following the success of *Gigi* and other novels by the French writer Sidonie Gabrielle Colette, known simply as Colette.

Colleen: Girl. An Irish name which is now found more in the US than in Ireland. Other forms: Coleen, Coline.

Constance: Loyal and firm. A name favoured by early Christians and then the Victorians. Other form: Connie.

Coral: Small stone. Coral jewellery became fashionable in Victorian England, and led to the word being adopted as one of the Edwardian jewel names at the turn of the century.

Cordelia: Heart. The Celtic name given to King Lear's third and only loving daughter in Shakespeare's tragedy, is probably derived from a German martyr named Cordula.

Corinna: Young girl. The beautiful and talented Greek poetess was one of the exceptional women of ancient Greece. Other forms: Cora, Coralie, Corinne, Kora.

Cressida: In *Troilus and Cressida*, Shakespeare followed medieval tradition and named the woman who forsook her Trojan lover for the Greek enemy Cressida rather than the original name Briseis.

Crystal: Ice. The Greek word came to be used for the hard, brilliant rock and was therefore a popular Edwardian jewel name. Other forms: Christel, Chrystal.

Cynthia: Artemis, the Greek goddess of the moon, was sometimes called Cynthia, and Tudor poets praised Elizabeth I with this name. Popular from the 1920s, but now usually given as the shortened form Cindy, especially in the US. Other forms: Cinda, Cynthiana, Sindy.

Daisy: Day's eye. The yellow-centred flower opens its white petals by day, closes them by night. This and Marguerite, the French word for daisy, were popular Victorian flower names.

Dana: God is my judge. This female form of Daniel was introduced to Britain from Scandinavia. Other forms: Danella, Dania.

Daphne: Laurel. When the Greek goddess of music and poetry fled from Apollo's arms, he transformed her into a laurel bush. A popular name this century.

Davina: Loved by God. The Scottish female form of David. Other forms: Davida, Davita, Devina, Vita.

Dawn: Break of day. A name which replaced its Latin equivalent Aurora this century, and was encouraged by Dawn Addams who starred with Charlie Chaplin in *A King in New York* (1957).

Deborah: A bee. The Hebrew word implied wisdom, eloquence and female perfection. A Puritan favourite, revived this century and made more popular by the British actress Deborah Kerr. Other forms: Debbie, Debo, Debra.

Deirdre: Broken-hearted. In Irish mythology, the beautiful Deirdre eloped from Ulster to Scotland only to commit suicide after her lover was murdered by the king.

Delia: The Greek name for the goddess of the moon, Artemis, who was born on Mount Kynthos on the island of Delos.

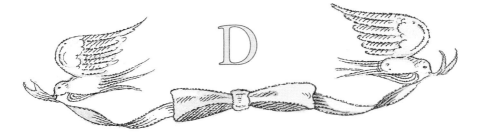

Denise: Lame god. A French name, popular in the Middle Ages and back in favour this century. Other forms: Denice, Denis, Denyse.

Diana: Divine. The Roman goddess of the woodlands, the moon, hunting and wild animals was also the goddess of chastity. The name became very fashionable when the Prince of Wales married Lady Diana Frances Spencer in 1981. Other forms: Diane, Dianna, Dianne, Didi, Diona.

Dilys: Sincere, genuine. A Welsh name used in Wales and England since the mid-19th century.

Dinah: Judged. A biblical name – the beautiful daughter of Jacob and Leah – revived this century.

Donna: Lady. An Italian name, implying a woman worthy of respect. Its use in Britain now follows its popularity in the US in the 1950s.

Doreen: Gift. Probably a form of Dora, the name became popular in the 1920s.

Doris: Of the ocean. In Greek mythology, the daughter of Oceanus, god of the sea, and wife of Nereus to whom she bore 50 golden-haired sea-nymphs. An Edwardian favourite, unusual now.

Dorothy: Gift of God. Used since the 15th century, it gained popularity in the 1930s with Dorothy in *The Wizard of Oz*. Also the generic name for a child's doll. Theodora is the name Dorothea in reverse. Other forms: Dodo, Doll, Dora, Dorita, Dorothea, Dottie.

Ebony: Ebony wood. A name implying strength, value and durability.

Edith: Successful in war. A royal Anglo-Saxon name that survived the Norman Conquest and became one of the most popular names in the 1880s, when it was given to the actress Dame Edith Evans (1888–1976). Other forms: Ardith, Eadita, Eady, Edie.

Edwina: Prosperous friend. This female form of Edwin is mostly found in Scotland. Other forms: Edwena, Edwyna.

Eileen: Life-giving, light-giving. Developed from the Irish Eibhlin and Ailbhlin, forms of Eve and Helen. Arriving in England with other Irish names in the 1870s, it became a British favourite until the 1950s. Aileen is the Scottish form. Other forms: Eilean, Eilleen, Elain, Elaine, Ilene.

Elaine: *See* Eileen.

Eleanor: Pity, mercy. A French name probably related to the Italian Eleonora, and brought to Britain by Henry II's bride, Eleanor of Aquitaine. Charles II's favourite was Elinor – or Nell–Gwyn, and Dickens used this form for his heroine Little Nell in *The Old Curiosity Shop*. Other forms: Ella, Ellen, Leonora, Nora, Norah, Noreen.

Elizabeth: God's oath, God's satisfaction. A name that has biblical, saintly and royal associations. Popular since Elizabeth I's reign, it gained many forms, including Lilibet, the childhood nickname for Elizabeth II who was christened Elizabeth Alexandra Mary in 1926. Of names announced in *The Times* newspaper, Elizabeth has been the favourite for the past 11 years. Other forms: Bess, Beth, Betsey, Bettina, Elisabet, Elisabeth, Elsa, Elspeth, Isabel, Libby, Lisa, Lisbet, Lizette.

Ella: Entirely, all. An Old German name revived by the Victorians, and famous today through the American singer Ella Fitzgerald.

Elsa: Noble maiden. The heroine of Richard Wagner's opera, *Lohengrin*, revived the medieval name last century. The actress Elsa Lanchester (1902–86) has helped to keep it popular.

Elspeth: *See* Elizabeth.

Elvira: Wise advice. A Spanish name used for the heroines of Mozart's *Don Giovanni*, of Molière's *Don Juan*, and of the Swedish film *Elvira Madigan*.

Emily: Industrious, earnest work. The English form of Amelia, was particularly popular in the 19th century, and is coming back into fashion now. Other forms: Emaline, Emilia, Emma, Milly.

Emma: All-embracing. Queen Emma of Normandy married first King Ethelred of England, then his successor, Knute. Revived during last century by Jane Austen's novel of that name and Flaubert's *Madame Bovary*.

Esme: *See* Amy.
Estelle: Star. A French name first found in Britain as Charles Dickens' heroine, Estella, in *Great Expectations* (1861). Other forms: Estel, Stella.
Esther: Star. A Persian name given to the Babylonian goddess of love. During its popularity from the 17th to the 19th century, it was interchangeable with Hester.
Eulalia: Sweet speech. A name given to Apollo, the Greek god of sun and light who made crops ripen and protected animals. Also the name of a celebrated Spanish saint.
Eve: Life-giving. As the name of the first woman and mother in the Bible, it was believed to bring longevity. Other forms: Eva, Evalina, Evelyn, Evita, Zoe.
Evelyn: Hazelnut, fruit of wisdom. A name given to girls and boys. Introduced by the Normans, it also has Celtic associations. Other forms: Avelina, Eve, Evelina, Evonne.

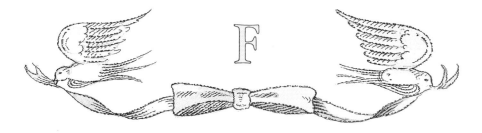

Faith: Devotion, trust. Faith, Hope and Charity are the three principal Christian virtues. The Puritans adopted all three names, together with others, such as Constance, Patience and Grace.

Fanny: Independent. Although it can be a shortened form of Frances, it gained popularity in its own right in the 1950s. *See also* Myfanwy.

Fay: Fidelity. A French name that has become popular this century, helped by a string of popular writers and actresses: Fay Compton, Fay Wray, Fay Bainter, Faye Emerson and Faye Dunaway.

Felicity: Good fortune. The Roman goddess of good luck became known in Britain as Felice, until the popularity of Felicia in the last century and Felicity in this.

Fiona: Fair, white. The Celtic name Fionn only came into general use as Fiona this century, becoming extremely fashionable in 1950s Scotland, then in 1970s England. Other forms: Fenella, Finola, Fionna.

Flavia: Yellow, blonde. A common Roman name that was taken up by the French as Flavie, by the Spanish and Italians as Flavia.

Fleur: Flower. The French name given to Soames Forsyte's daughter, their 'petite fleur', in John Galsworthy's *The Forsyte Saga* (1906–21).

Flora: Flower. The name of the Roman goddess of spring was used in Scotland to honour the Jacobite heroine Flora MacDonald, who helped the Young Pretender escape to France after the Battle of Culloden (1746). Other forms: Flore, Florella, Floris.

Florence: Flourishing. Originally given to girls and boys in the Middle Ages to honour St Florentius. The nurse Florence Nightingale (1820–1910) was named after the Italian city where she was born, and her medical reforms ensured the name was honoured from that time.

Frances: Independent. St Frances Cabrini, who helped Italian immigrants in America, was in 1950 the first American to be canonised and is patron of emigrants. A popular name since the 18th century. Other forms: Fanny, Fran, Francesca, Francine, Frankie.

Frederica: Gentle ruler. This female form of Frederick was brought to Britain by the Hanoverian kings, remaining popular with the Victorians.

Freya: Noble lady. Freja was the Norse goddess of love and fertility.

Frieda: Peace. An Old German name, either used as a short form of Frederica or Elfrieda, or independently.

G

Gabriella: God's heroine. This Italian female form of Gabriel has been gaining favour in Britain since the 1950s. Other forms: Gabby, Gabriele, Gavi.

Gail: A father's happiness. Now fully independent of Abigail, having suddenly become popular in the 1940s. Other forms: Gael, Gale, Gayle.

Gemma: Precious stone, gem. This Italian name honouring St Gemma Galgani is now one of the top 50 British names. Other forms: Gemmer, Jemma.

Genevieve: Womankind. In France, a name honouring the patron saint of Paris. In Britain, a name more likely to be associated with the veteran car in the film *Genevieve* (1953).

Georgina: Labourer. A female version of George, created under the Hanoverian kings and fashionable ever since, especially in Scotland. Other forms: Georgette, Georgia, Georgiana, Georgie.

Geraldine: Ruler by spear. The Earl of Surrey (1517–47) made up the name for his love poems dedicated to Lady Elizabeth Fitzgerald. Both Geraldine and Gerald were 1950s favourites.

Gertrude: Spear-strength. A name that rose to popularity late last century, at the time that actress Gertrude Lawrence (1898–1952) and writer Gertrude Stein (1874–1946) were born. Other forms: Gerda, Trudy.

Gillian: *See* Julia.

Gladys: Princess, queen, ruler. The Welsh name Gwladys acquired this highly fashionable, anglicised form late last century and remained popular until the 1930s.

Glenda: Holy goodness. This Welsh name was rarely found in Britain before the 1930s, although it was common in the US and Australia.

Glenys: Fair, holy. A Welsh name especially popular during the 1950s. Other forms: Glennis, Glennys.

G

Gloria: Fame, honour. The name was originally Gloriosa, then Gloriana to honour Elizabeth I. In the late 19th century Shaw called the heroine of *You Never Can Tell* (1898) Gloria. This century, the actress Gloria Swanson preferred it to her real name, Josephine.

Grace: Natural charm. Associated with the three graces of Greek mythology, it was a fashionable Victorian name. The music hall singer Gracie Fields, and the actress Grace Kelly, who became Princess Grace of Monaco, have kept the name in vogue this century.

Griselda: Grey warrior. A German name still associated with the exemplary, patient wife in Giovanni Boccaccio's *Decameron* (1348–53), later retold by Chaucer in *The Clerk's Tale*. Other forms: Grizelda, Grizzel, Zelda.

Gwendoline: Blessed circle. Gwendolen was the Celtic moon goddess and the name of King Arthur's legendary beloved. A Welsh name popularised by George Eliot's novel *Daniel Deronda* (1874–6). Other forms: Gwen, Gwenda, Gwendolen.

Gwyneth: Blessed with happiness. A Welsh name popular in Britain between the World Wars. As Gwynedd, it is the Welsh name for North Wales. Other forms: Gwenyth, Gwynneth.

Hannah: God's favour. An Old Testament name given to Samuel's mother. Especially popular during and after the Reformation, it is now coming back into fashion again. Other forms: Anna, Anne, Hanna, Nana.

Harriet: Ruler of the home. This female version of Harry has been popular since the Middle Ages. Henrietta was given royal distinction by Charles II's French queen, Henrietta Maria, who was named after her father Henry. More recently, the name of the author of *Uncle Tom's Cabin* (1852), Harriet Beecher Stowe. Other forms: Ettie, Harrie, Hattie.

Hayley: Hay-meadow. A name made popular in the 1960s by the child actress Hayley Mills who starred in *Tiger Bay* (1959) and won an Oscar for *Pollyanna* the following year.

Hazel: Hazelnut. Popular with the Victorians who favoured flower names. The ancient hazel-wand symbolised wisdom and protection.

Heather: The mauve-flowering heathland shrub thrives in northern England and Scotland and the name has been popular throughout Britain this century.

Helen: Light-giving. A consistently popular name, encouraged by the beautiful Greek heroine who was thought to be the most beautiful of women, and by the deaf and blind Helen Keller who learnt to speak, read and write. Other forms: Eileen, Ellen, Helena, Nelly.

Henrietta: *See* Harriet.

Hermione: The female version of Hermes, messenger of the Greek gods, who also protected travellers. Another form, Hermia, appears in Shakespeare's *A Midsummer Night's Dream* and in the novels of Sir Walter Scott.

Hester: *See* Esther.

Hilary: Cheerful. A name given to boys until the 17th century, then revived by the Victorians for both sexes. Other forms: Hilaire, Hillary.

Hilda: Battle. The 7th-century abbess of Whitby, St Hilda, has kept this name popular in the north of England.

Holly: Holly-tree. It is the bright red berries of the tree that symbolise life and give this name added meaning. In John Galsworthy's *The Forsyte Saga* (1906–21), Jolly and Holly are brother and sister.

Honor: Acknowledge, respect. Favoured by the Puritans as the virtue, Honour, it has been popularised today by the 1960s star Honor Blackman.

Hope: Optimistic wish. As one of the three fundamental Christian virtues – Faith, Hope and Charity – this was a Puritan favourite given to both sexes.

Ida: To toil. Came into fashion in the last century when Gilbert and Sullivan adapted Tennyson's poem *The Princess* for their operetta *Princess Ida* (1880).

Imogen: Likeness. The romantic heroine of Shakespeare's *Cymbeline*, a play about the ancient British ruler whose kingdom covered what is now the county of Hertfordshire. Other forms: Emogene, Imo, Imogene.

Ingrid: Meadow. Ing was the Norse god of fertility and Ingrid (Ing's ride) was the boar he rode. A name made more popular in Britain in recent years through the Swedish actress Ingrid Bergman. Other forms: Inga, Inge, Inky.

Irene: Peace. The gentle name for the Greek goddess of peace was taken up last century and was given to one of the principal characters in John Galsworthy's *The Forsyte Saga*. Promoted this century by Irene Dunne's performance in the musical *Showboat* (1929), later filmed.

Iris: Rainbow. This favourite Victorian flower name refers to the Greek goddess of the rainbow who carried messages from gods to mortals across her multicoloured bridge.

Isabel: God's satisfaction. This Spanish and Portuguese form of Elizabeth was also popular in France and Scotland in the Middle Ages and was only surpassed in popularity by the Italian form, Isabella, last century. Other forms: Belita, Isabelle.

Isadora: Gift of Isis. A Greek name referring to the Egyptian goddess of the moon and fertility. The dancer Isadora Duncan (1878–1927) encouraged the name this century.

Jacqueline: Supplanter. This French female form of Jacob came to Britain with Henry V's sister-in-law, whose nickname was Jack. This century, its peak of popularity and variety of spellings was in the 1950s. Other forms: Jacolyn, Jacqualine, Jacquelyne.

Jade: Nephrite, jadite. The French word for two translucent, blue-green gemstones is now gaining popularity.

Jane: God's mercy. The female form of John. In the Middle Ages Joan was used, but the Tudors preferred Jane which has remained a top favourite ever since. Other forms: Jaine, Jancis, Janet, Janice, Janine, Jayne, Jean, Jessie, Joanna, Sheena.

Janet: God's mercy. Scotland's links with France encouraged this Scottish form of

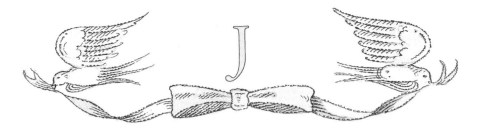

Jane, developed from the French version, Jeannette. Other forms: Janette, Jenny.

Jasmine: Olive flower. The Persian word for the sweet-smelling jasmine flowers was fashionable with the Victorians, revived in the 1930s and is still popular today.

Jean: God's mercy. Like Janet, a popular Scottish form of Jane taken from a French version, this time Jehane. Popular in Britain during the 1930s, when the actress Jean Simmons was born. Other forms: Gene, Jeanette, Jeanine, Jenny.

Jemima: Dove. A biblical name, belonging to one of patient Job's beautiful daughters, it is the female form of Benjamin. Now associated with the duck in Beatrix Potter's children's story, *The Tale of Jemima Puddle-Duck* (1908).

Jennifer: Fair, smooth. This English version of the Welsh name Guinevere only moved out of Cornwall in the 1920s to become a British favourite by 1950. Other forms: Gaynor, Ginevra, Guenevere, Jenifer, Jenny, Wander.

Jessica: God beholds. The female form of Jesse who, in the Bible, was father of King David. The name of Shylock's daughter in Shakespeare's *Merchant of Venice*, it was considered a Jewish name until recently.

Jessie: *See* Jane.

Jill: *See* Julia.

Joan: *See* Joanna.

Joanna: God's mercy. Another form of Jane, this time the Old Latin name Johanna contracted to Joan, then lengthened again. This, and the French form Joanne, are both in the 1980s' British top 50 names.

Jocelin: Of the Goths. A name referring to the German people, it was introduced by the Normans and given only to boys until this century. Other forms: Jocelyn, Josceline, Joscelyn.

Jodie: Praise. This form of Judith, popularised in the US this century, is now in the 1980s' British top 50 names.

Joelle: God's willingness. The French female form of Joel, and the name of several Old Testament figures.

Josephine: God multiplies. The French female version of Joseph has been a popular Catholic choice since the pope created the festival of St Joseph on March 19, 1621. Introduced into Britain when Napoleon used it as a nickname for his wife, Empress Marie Josephe Rose (1763–1814). Other forms: Fifine, Jodie, Jospha, Pepita.

Joy: Merriment. A medieval name toned down by the Puritans to Joy-in-Sorrow, then restored to simplicity and popularity by the Victorians.

Joyce: Joyful. Adapted from the French name Joisse. The 7th-century Breton saint popularised the name for boys, but girls also benefited from its Victorian revival.

J-K

Judith: Praise. The apocryphal story of brave Judith slaying the enemy general, Holophernes, may have inspired Shakespeare to choose it for one of his daughters. Others forms: Jodie, Jody, Judy.

Julia: Fair-skinned. Juliana and Gillian were the medieval versions; Juliet the Tudor addition; and Julia became popular in the early 18th century. Julie is now more common. Other forms: Gill, Jill, Jillian.

Juliet: Fair-skinned. The anglicised version of the Italian name Giulietta was used by Shakespeare for his tragedy *Romeo and Juliet* set in the Italian town of Verona.

June: Young. June was mother of the Roman god of war, Mars. As the name of the month it originates from the important Roman family, Junius.

Karen: Pure. This Danish form of Katerina, from Catherine, gained favour in the 1960s, together with the similar sounding names Sharon and Darren.

Katherine, Kathleen: *See* Catherine and Caitlin.

Katie: Pure. This form of Catherine is now in the 1980s' British top 20 names, perhaps still influenced by the volatile Kate of Shakespeare's *The Taming of the Shrew* and Susan M. Coolidge's *What Katy Did* novels. Other forms: Kate, Katy.

Kay: Rejoice. Popular only since the 1930s. Chosen by the British actress Kay Kendall in favour of her real name, Justine, and boosted by her popularity . *See also* Catherine.

Kelly: Warlike. This anglicised form of the Irish name Cealach has recently become popular and is now among the top 10 favourite names. Other forms: Kayley, Kealy, Kellie, Kerley, Kylie.

Kerry: Dark one. From the Irish Gaelic, is the name given to the south-west county of Ireland. Adopted as a name this century, first for boys, then for girls.

Kirsty: Anointed. The Scottish familiar form of Christine spread further afield after World War II to enjoy instant popularity. Other forms: Kerstin, Kirstie.

Kylie: Curl. Used by the Australian Aborigines to describe a boomerang; by the 1970s this was Australia's third favourite girls' name. *See also* Kelly.

Larissa: Hilarious, playful. A new name in Britain, possibly introduced from Russia. Other forms: Larisa, Larry.

Laura: Laurel. For the Greeks and Romans, a laurel-wreath was a symbol of outstanding achievement. A name revived in the 1940s with the help of the popular song, and Otto Preminger's film *Laura*. Other forms: Lauren, Loraine, Lorna.

Lauren: Laurel. This form of Laura, also possibly a female form of Lawrence, was chosen by Howard Hawks in the 1940s as the stage name for his new actress Betty Jean Bacall. She made it instantly fashionable, particularly in the US.

Lavender: The fragrant, pale mauve flowers made this an especially appealing Victorian flower name.

Lavinia: A favourite with the Tudors and Hanoverians because of its classical associations with the wife of Aeneas, the Roman who linked the mortals to their gods through his mother, the goddess Aphrodite.

Leanne: Lion woman. This female version of Leander, the Greek hero who nightly swam the Hellespont to visit his beloved, has shot into the 1980s' British top 20 girls' names.

Leonora: Pity, mercy. This operatic favourite, an Italian short form of Eleonora, was the name of the heroine in Beethoven's *Fidelio* and Verdi's *Il Trovatore*. Other forms: Leanora, Nora.

Lesley: Low-lying meadow. Robert Burns (1759–96) took the old Aberdeenshire family name and gave it to 'bonnie Lesley' in one of his poems. Leslie, for boys, came later and when both forms were popular this century, Humphrey Bogart named his daughter after Leslie Howard.

Lillian: Lily. The bloom that symbolises purity, it was a popular Victorian flower name. The American actress Lillian Gish, together with the American writer Lillian Hellman, gave it some popularity this century. Other forms: Lilian, Lily.

Linda: Snake. With its Scandinavian associations with wisdom and immortality, Linda gained independence from Belinda and Melinda last century and was most popular in the 1950s. Other forms: Lindy, Lynda.

Lindsay: Linden tree. The family name of the Scottish Earls of Crawford emerged as a common first name for girls in the 1930s, soon becoming even more of a favourite than the boy's name.

Lisa: God's oath. This short form of Elizabeth is now an independent name and among the top 10 favourite girls' names of the 1980s.

Lois: Good, worthy of desire. As a more unusual biblical name signifying virtue, the Puritans took it up and then carried it to the US where it enjoys greatest popularity today.

Lorna: R. D. Blackmore gave the Scottish place name Lorn to the heroine of his bestselling romantic novel, *Lorna Doone* (1869), thus encouraging its popularity in Scotland. Other forms: Lona, Lorne.

Lorraine: Two influential women from this area of France encouraged use of the name, particularly in Scotland: they were Jeanne la Lorraine, known as Joan of Arc, and the mother of Mary Queen of Scots. Other forms: Lora, Lorrain.

Louise: Glorious in war. This female form of the French Louis rose to popularity under the Stuarts – often as Louisa – and is still popular today. Other forms: Eloisa, Heloise, Lois, Lolita, Lulu.

Lucinda: Shining out. This form of Lucy gained favour in the 18th century, with other similar sounding names such as Belinda. Other forms: Cindy, Lucille.

Lucy: Shining out. St Lucy, the Sicilian martyr who had her eyes plucked out, is the patron saint of eye diseases. A popular name in the Middle Ages, it gave way to Lucia in the 17th century. More recently, the American Lucy Stone (1818–93) campaigned for women's rights. The form Lucia was used by E. F. Benson in his 1920s stories of Mapp and Lucia.

Lucretia: The Roman woman who committed suicide in shame after Tarquinius raped her, not the infamous Lucretia Borgia, gave this name its associations with virgin purity.

Lynette: Idol. The Old French form of the Welsh name Eiluned was used by Tennyson in his Arthurian romance of Lynette and Gareth in *Idylls of the King* (1859). Other forms: Linette, Linnet, Lynetta.

Lynn: Brook. This Old English name, also given to boys, has become popular again this century with several film actresses – Lynn Fontanne, Lynn Bari and Lynn Redgrave.

Mabel: Lovable. This short form of Amabel was a Victorian and Edwardian favourite in its own right. Other forms: Mabbs, Mabelle, Mable, Mapps.

Madeleine: Lofty tower. St Mary Magdalene, the patroness of penitents, probably came from Magdala, a city famed for its tower. This original French form is now preferred to the British version, Madeline. Other forms: Marla, Marleen, Marlene.

Maeve: An anglicised version of Meadhbh – the name of a 1st-century Irish queen – is still popular in Ireland.

Maida: Unmarried girl. This and Maidie enjoyed Victorian and Edwardian popularity, to be revived in the 1960s.

Maisie: Pearl. A short form of Margery, the Scottish form of Margaret, which enjoyed popularity in the 1920s and '30s.

Marcella: Shining. The female form of Mark, promoted by the beautiful woman in Cervantes' *Don Quixote* (1605) who bewitched all young men and then rejected them.

Margaret: Pearl. A consistently popular name, especially in Scotland, with countless variations. The many saintly and royal bearers of the name range from the medieval queen and saint, Margaret of Scotland, to the present Queen's sister, Margaret Rose. Other forms: Daisy, Greta, Madge, Mae, Maggie, Maisie, Margarita, Margery, Marghanita, Margot, Marjorie, Mog, Molly, Peggy, Polly, Rita.

Marigold: Mary's gold. A flower name that has remained popular this century, perhaps because Mary refers to the Virgin.

Marilyn: Mary's line. The name refers to descendants of the Virgin Mary. The 1920s' music-hall singer Marilyn Miller inspired Norma Jean Baker's agent to choose the name Marilyn Monroe for the actress who became the 1950s' sex symbol.

Marion: Another Mary name, this time from the French form Marie. Arriving with the Normans, it became a popular folklore name and was given to the hero Robin Hood's companion, Maid Marion.

Martha: Household mistress. The biblical figure who complained of her household chores to Jesus, is patroness of housewives. Has enjoyed some popularity in Britain since the 18th century, but is now more common in the US.

Martina: Warlike. The female form of the French name Martin only became common in the 1950s.

Mary: The most important Christian female name derives from Miriam, which has no clear meaning. The Virgin Mary, mother of Jesus Christ, inspired a cult so fervent that the name was sometimes considered too holy to use. But after the 12th century it became the most consistently popular name in Europe, either as the Mediterranean Maria, the French Marie, the Welsh Mair or the Irish Moira and Maureen. Other forms: Marion, Maura, May, Mia, Mimi, Minnie, Mira, Mitzi, Molly, Moyra.

Matilda: Strong in battle. The name of William the Conqueror's wife was revived by the Victorians. The Australian slang, Waltzing Matilda, means carrying one's possessions in a bundle, not dancing with a pretty girl. Other form: Mathilda.

Maud: Strong in battle. William the Conqueror's granddaughter, Matilda, was known as Maud. Its popularity in the last century was helped by the song of Tennyson's poem, 'Come into the Garden, Maud'.

Maureen: *See* Mary.

Mavis: Song-thrush. The Old French word used by poets was only taken up as a Christian name in the last century.

Maxime: Greatest. This female form of Maximillian, popular with the Romans as Maxima, has been used increasingly in Britain since the 1930s.

May: The Romans named the spring month after Maia, their Earth Mother, whom they honoured with festivities on May Day. *See also* Mary. Other forms: Mae, Mai, Maya.

Melanie: Dark complexion. The athletic Greek god Melanion won his beloved Atalanta's hand by beating her in a running race. The female form, imported from France, gained popularity through Margaret Mitchell's *Gone with the Wind* (1936).

Melissa: Bee. A name with honey-sweet associations that arrived from Italy in the 18th century. Other forms: Melisa, Misha.

Meryl: *See* Muriel.

Michelle: Who can be like God? This form of the French female version of Michael has gained enormous popularity in Britain since the 1950s, perhaps helped by The Beatles' ballad.

Mildred: Gentle strength. An 8th-century Milthryth was one of three sisters who all became saints. Gained favour under the Hanoverians and later with the Victorians who liked medieval names.

Millicent: Noble determination. The Normans brought the French fairy name Melisande to Britain, but Millicent only became popular in the last century.

Miranda: To astonish. The name used by Shakespeare for the heroine of his play *The Tempest*.

Miriam: This Hebrew name, the original form of Mary, is first mentioned in the Bible as Moses' sister. Found in Britain since the 7th century, its meaning is still uncertain.

Moira: *See* Mary.

Molly: *See* Margaret *and* Mary.

Mona: Noble, angel or nun. The anglicised form of the Irish name Muadhnait came into vogue in both England and Ireland in the last century. People who live on the Isle of Man know it as the Latin name for their island.

Morag: Sun. A Gaelic name found mostly in Scotland. The name is also thought to be a Gaelic form of Sarah.

Muriel: Sparkling like the sea. The ancient Irish name Muirgheal was used in Brittany, Wales and Ireland. A medieval favourite, revived by the Victorians. Other forms: Meriel, Meryl, Meryle.

Myfanwy: My rare treasure. A Welsh name popular since the last century, its English form is Fanny.

Myrna: Gentle. This Gaelic name was given prominence by the Hollywood star Myrna Loy in the 1930s.

Nadia: Hope. This Russian name was popularised by Lenin's wife, although it had come to Britain last century with Olga, Sonia, Vera and other Russian names. The French version is Nadine.

Nancy: Fortunate. This form of Anne gained independent status after the reign of Queen Anne (1702–14). It came into the limelight this century with Nancy Astor (1879–1964) who in 1919 became the first woman to sit as a member of the House of Commons.

Naomi: Delightful. A natural Puritan choice, with its pleasant meaning and its biblical associations with the long-suffering mother-in-law of Ruth.

Natalie: Birth, birthday. This French name is also popular in its Russian form, Natasha, the name of the heroine of Tolstoy's *War and Peace* (1865–9). Other forms: Natalia, Nathalie, Noel.

Nicola: The people's triumph. The Italian female form of Nicholas, known in medieval Britain, joined the top 10 favourites this century. The French forms, Nicole and Nicolette, are less common. Other forms: Nicki, Nicolina, Nikki.

Nina: Young girl. The Spanish word was also the short form of the Russian name Annina.

Noelle: Christmas. This French name is apt for a Christmas baby.

Nora, Norah: *See* Eleanor, Leonora.

Norma: Carpenter's pattern. The princess heroine of Bellini's opera *Norma* (1831) promoted the name, and in the 1930s and '40s the American actress Norma Shearer made it popular again.

Octavia: Eight. The sister of the Roman Emperor Augustus was forsaken by her husband Mark Antony, who was bewitched by the beautiful Cleopatra.

Olga: Holy. This Russian name derives from Helga, an Old Norse name. It came to Britain in the last century.

Olivia: Olive. The name symbolising peace was fashionable in the Renaissance and popularised by Shakespeare in *Twelfth Night*, Oliver Goldsmith's *The Vicar of Wakefield* (1766) and *The Good Natured Man* (1768), and recently by the film actress Olivia de Havilland who starred as Melanie in *Gone with the Wind* (1939). Other forms: Livia, Livvy, Nollie, Olive.

Ophelia: Help. A name popular with Victorians more for its medieval origins than for the fate of the beautiful heroine in Shakespeare's *Hamlet*.

Paloma: Dove. Like the olive, a symbol of peace. The painter Picasso gave this Spanish name to his daughter.

Pamela: All honey-sweet. Possibly invented by Sir Philip Sidney (1554–86) for a romantic epic. Popularised by Samuel Richardson's bestselling romance, *Pamela, or a Virtue Rewarded* (1740).

Pandora: Multi-gifted. In Greek mythology each god gave Pandora a power to bring about the downfall of man. When her husband opened Jupiter's present, a box, the evils of the world flew out.

Pascale: Pass over. The French name refers to the Passover or to Easter, so it is apt for an Easter baby. The Cornish names Pascow and Pascoe reflect the Cornish word for Easter, Pask.

Patience: Sufferer. With its implications of calm endurance, a favourite Puritan name that has remained in use since the 17th century.

Patricia: Aristocrat. This female form of Patrick came to England from Scotland, not Ireland, and was popularised by Princess Patricia of Connaught, who was Queen Victoria's granddaughter and known as Pat. Other forms: Patti, Tricia.

Paula: Small. This female version of Paul arrived from Germany in the 1920s and became a 1950s favourite. Other forms: Pauleen, Paulette, Pauline.

Peggy: *See* Margaret.

Penelope: Weaver. In Greek mythology Odysseus returned from travelling to find his faithful wife Penelope had craftily repelled her suitors. She promised to select one when she had finished her weaving, but secretly unpicked her day's work each night. Other form: Penny.

Philippa: Horse-loving. Edward III's queen brought the Greek name to Britain in the 14th century, but it was written without the final 'a' until Victorian times. Other forms: Phil, Pippa.

Philomena: Song-lover. In Greek mythology the gods saved the Athenian princess, Philomena, from the clutches of the Thracian king by transforming her into a nightingale.

Phoebe: Shining. The name of the Greek goddess of the moon, popular with the Hanoverians and Victorians but unusual now. Other forms: Phebe, Pheby.

Phyllis: Foliage. A favourite name with classical poets for country sweethearts, referring to the Greek maiden who pined for her beloved and was transformed into an almond tree. Other form: Phillida.

Pia: Dutiful. This name, implying piousness and faithfulness, is now gaining popularity.

Polly: A rhyming variation of Molly, a short form of both Margaret and Mary. Used independently since the 18th century, when John Gay chose it for the heroine of *The Beggar's Opera* (1727).

Poppy: A Victorian flower name now enjoying a revival.

Portia: Hog. In *The Merchant of Venice*, Shakespeare gave this Roman family name to his clever heroine who posed as a lawyer to save Antonio's life.

Primrose: Early rose. The delicate, pale yellow blossoms made this a particularly popular Victorian flower name.

Priscilla: Strict. A favourite with the Puritans for its association with discipline and austerity. Other forms: Cilla, Precilla.

Prudence: Sensible, discreet. Current since the Middle Ages, it became an early Puritan favourite. Later used by Lord Lytton in his novel *The Sea Captain* (1839) for the woman who protects his heroine from strange men.

Prunella: Little plum. A name imported from France last century, to enjoy great popularity in Britain in the 1930s.

Queenie: Woman companion. The name implies the supreme woman, whether she is queen of a man's heart, a house or a realm. Used as an affectionate first name for Queen Victoria and then by the Edwardians.

Rachel: Ewe. A biblical name given to Jacob's wife and symbolising innocence. Used since the Reformation but only now gaining real popularity.

Rebecca: Knotted cord. The name of Isaac's beautiful wife in the Old Testament implies faithfulness. Kate Douglas's *Rebecca of Sunnybrook Farm* (1903), the novelist Rebecca West, and Alfred Hitchcock's film (1940) of Daphne du Maurier's novel *Rebecca* all helped to popularise the name which is now in the 1980s' top 10. Other forms: Becca, Beckie.

Regina: Queen, mistress. Used in the Middle Ages to describe the Virgin Mary; revived by the Victorians for their queen, and now used as a first name.

Rhoda: Rose. This Roman name referred to Rhodes, island of roses. Popular last century, and recently revived.

Rhona: Rough isle. Probably a Scottish place name adopted as a first name and popular in Scotland late last century.

Rita: Pearl. A form of Margaret that rose to popularity in the 1930s when the actress Margarita Cansino made several films before changing her name to Rita Hayworth.

Roberta: Illustrious fame. This female form of Robert appeared in the last century and was boosted by Jerome Kern's musical *Roberta* (1934), starring Ginger Rogers. Other forms: Bobby, Robin, Robina, Robyn, Ruby.

Rosalie: Feast of roses. The Rosalia was the annual Roman ceremony of hanging rose-garlands on tombs.

Rosalind: Horse-serpent. This is a German name adopted by the Spanish who translated it as pretty rose, as if it was Spanish. Introduced by the Normans; popularised by Shakespeare's heroine in *As You Like It*. Other form: Rosaleen.

Rosamond: Protector of horses. Like Rosalind, the German Rosamond underwent a radical change of meaning, this time to rose of the world as if its origins were Latin.

Rose: Although, like Rosamond, the name probably derives from the German for horse, the flower symbolised a beautiful maiden in the medieval French romance *Roman de la Rose*, and has come to be synonymous with love and beauty.

Rosemary: Dew of the sea. A Victorian flower name that has remained in vogue.

Rowena: Fair and slender. The anglicised form of the Welsh name Rhonwen, chosen by Sir Walter Scott for the heroine of *Ivanhoe* (1819).

Roxanna: Dawn light. The Persian name of Alexander the Great's jealous wife who stabbed her rival. Other form: Roxanne.

Ruth: Companion. The biblical Ruth left her homeland to become the unhappy but loyal daughter-in-law of Naomi. Thus it was a favourite Puritan choice, especially for those who migrated to the US.

Sabrina: A name for the River Severn, possibly inspired by the Celtic legend of Sabrina, daughter of King Locrine and his mistress Estrildis, whose birth caused the queen to slay her husband and toss mother and daughter into this river.

Sally: Princess. This form of Sarah was a Hanoverian favourite, becoming popular again in the 1960s.

Samantha: Heard. A name implying the granting of parents' prayers for a child. A popular name in the US, crossing to Britain with the film *High Society* (1950), which includes Cole Porter's song 'I Love You, Samantha'.

Sarah: Princess. A favourite biblical name, given to Abraham's wife, which has been consistently fashionable since the Reformation. Morag is thought to be the Scottish form. Other forms: Sadie, Sallie, Sally, Sara, Sarai, Sarena, Zara, Zoreen.

Scarlett: Rich, reddish orange cloth. Probably a cloth-trader's surname turned first name. Katie Scarlett O'Hara, the heroine of Margaret Mitchell's *Gone with the Wind* (1936), was given her grandmother's maiden name.

Selina: Moon. The golden crown of the Greek goddess of the moon, also known as Artemisia and Phoebe, illuminated the skies as she crossed them nightly.

Serena: Calm and clear. Popular with early Christians in Rome, this name arrived in Britain in the 18th century.

Sharon: Plain. The name of the fertile plain lying between Jaffa and Mount Carmel in Israel. The heroine of Sinclair Lewis's novel *Elmer Gantry* (1927) promoted this biblical name, first in the US, then in Britain. Other forms: Shara, Shareen, Sharron, Sharyn.

Sheena: God's mercy. An anglicised form of the Gaelic name Sine, which is a form of Jean. Other forms: Sheenah, Shena.

Sheila: Divine place, heaven. Another anglicised name, this time from the Irish names Sile and Signile. Fashionable in the 1930s and still popular today. Other forms: Sheelah, Sheilah, Shelly.

Shirley: Bright meadow. This Yorkshire name was used by Charlotte Brontë for the heroine of her novel of that name. Popular again this century through the success of the child actress Shirley Temple, who starred in *Wee Willie Winkie* (1937) aged nine. Other form: Sherill.

Shona: God's mercy. An anglicised form of the Gaelic name Seonaid, the female form of Shaun.

Sibyl: Prophetess. The Romans believed that Sibyls' prophecies were inspired by the gods. A name revived last century, when it was given to the actress Dame Sybil Thorndike.

Simone: Snub-nosed. This French female form of Simon came to Britain in the 1940s, encouraged by the French actress Simone Signoret.

Sonia: Wisdom. This Russian form of Sophie arrived in Britain last century, with Olga, and other Russian names.

Sophie: Wisdom: This French form supplanted the original Greek form, Sophia, in the 1920s. The vaudeville star Sophie Tucker, born Sophia, promoted it in the 1930s.

Stacey: She will rise again. Now used as the Irish form of Anastasia, although it used to be the female form of Eustace.

Stella: Star. Popular with Roman Catholics because Stella Maris, star of the sea, is a name for the Virgin Mary. Also used by the poet Sir Philip Sidney (1554–86) to describe his beloved.

Stephanie: Crown. This French female form of Stephen, used by early Christians as Stephania, came to Britain in the 1920s. Other forms: Stefanie, Stephenie.

Susan: Lily. Susannah, the full name, was adopted by the Puritans, referring to the biblical Susannah falsely accused of adultery after she repelled the lecherous Elders. Not common until the 18th century, it gained popularity with the Victorians. Susan is now the favourite form. Other forms: Sukie, Susanna, Susanne, Susie, Suzanne, Suzannah, Suzie.

Sylvia: Wood. Rhea Silvia was the Roman goddess of nature and mother of Romulus and Remus. In Shakespeare's *Two Gentlemen of Verona* one gentleman's beloved is Silvia.

Tamsin: Twin. This female form of Thomas was popular in Cornwall before it became generally fashionable this century. Other forms: Tamasin, Tamsyn.

Tanya: Fairy queen. Titania, the queen of the fairies in Shakespeare's *A Midsummer Night's Dream*, is a character taken from a story related by the Roman poet Ovid. Tanya is the Russian form.

Tatum: Spirited. This female form of Tate has recently been encouraged by the film actress Tatum O'Neal who starred in the film *Paper Moon* (1973).

Teresa: To reap, harvest. This Greek name may also mean woman from Therasia. First made popular by St Teresa of Avila, and more recently by Mother Teresa who works for the homeless of the world. Other forms: Terese, Terry, Tess, Tessa, Theresa, Tracy.

Tessa: *See* Teresa.

Thea: Goddess. This Greek name, now fully independent, was originally a short form of Dorothea and Theodora.

Thelma: Will. A name invented by Marie Corelli for her bestseller, *Thelma: A Society Novel* (1887), then promoted by the American actress Thelma Ritter in the 1940s.

Theodora: Gift of God. First used by early Christians in Rome, this female form of Theodore is currently more popular than its reversed form, Dorothea. Other forms: Fedora, Thadine.

Thora: Thunderer. Thor was the Norse god of thunder and war, after whom Thursday, Thor's day, is named. A name found mostly in Lancashire, where the actress Thora Hird was born.

Tiffany: Divine manifestation. A name for girls and boys, derived from Epiphany, or Twelfth Night, when the Three Wise Men learnt of Christ's birth.

Tina: *See* Christine, Valentine.

Toyah: Whimsical, sporty. An Old English word that has only recently been given as a first name.

Tracy: To reap, harvest. This form of Teresa gained popularity with the film *High Society* (1950), in which Grace Kelly played the heiress, Tracy Samantha Lord. Other forms: Tracey, Trasey.

Tuesday: Tiw's day. The day of the week, only recently adopted as a first name, honours the Teutonic god of war.

Una: Lamb, or one. Implying innocence and purity, this Irish name was given to the woman for whom St George slayed the dragon. Other forms: Oonagh, Unity.

Ursula: She-bear. The name of the British medieval saint was used by Shakespeare in *Much Ado About Nothing*, then revived by the 1960s' Swiss sex symbol Ursula Andress.

Valentine: Strong, healthy. A name for both sexes, honouring the Roman saint martyred on February 13, the eve of the pagan festival for lovers. He was later remembered on the festival day, with its traditions. Other forms: Tina, Valentina.

Valerie: Strong, healthy. Derived from a Roman family name, it was introduced from France at the end of the last century and has grown in popularity since.

Vanessa: Star. A form of Esther, invented by Jonathan Swift to disguise Esther Vanhomrigh's name when he recounted their love affair in his poem *Cadenus and Vanessa* (1713).

Venetia: Mercy. The Italian region is named from the Veneti who lived in the area. Popularised by romantic literary heroines last century, as in Benjamin Disraeli's *Venetia* (1837).

Veronica: True image. The saint who wiped Christ's face as He carried the Cross and then found His image on the cloth is now patroness of photographers.

Vicki: Conqueror. This short form of Victoria is now fully independent and a top favourite choice. Other form: Vicky.

Victoria: Conqueror. First used by the Tudors as Victory before becoming highly fashionable in Queen Victoria's reign (1837–1901). Revived in the 1940s.

Violet: A flower that was a symbol of modesty in the Middle Ages. Long popular in Scotland, where it was influenced by the French form Violette, then a late Victorian favourite. Other forms: Viola, Violetta.

Virginia: Manly race. The name also has associations with maidenhood. Sir Walter Raleigh named the American state of Virginia after Elizabeth I, the virgin Queen. Became popular last century, with the success of Bernardin de Saint-Pierre's romance, *Paul et Virginie* (1787).

Vita: Life. Popularised this century by the novelist Vita Sackville-West, who created the gardens of Sissinghurst Castle. Also a form of Victoria.

Vivien: Full of life. The name of the witty enchantress of Arthurian legend was revived by Victorian medievalists and promoted this century by the actress Vivien Leigh, who changed the spelling from Vivian.

Wallis: Welshman. This female form of Wallace was made famous by the American, Mrs Wallis Simpson, for whom Edward VIII gave up the British throne.

Wanda: Vandal. A Slavonic name derived from the German tribe, the Vandals, called Wendlas by the Anglo-Saxons. A name more common in the US, only now gaining popularity in Britain.

Wendy: Friend. The writer James Barrie invented the name for the heroine of his play *Peter Pan: or The Boy Who Would Not Grow Up* (1904), inspired by his young friend, Margaret, who called him her 'fwendy-wendy'.

Winifred: Friend of peace. Although derived from the old name Winfrith, this is also the anglicised form of the Welsh name Gwenfrewi, meaning blessed reconciliation or white wave. Other forms: Freddie, Guenevere, Wynne.

Xanthe: Yellow. The name of the hero Achilles' horse, although its meaning makes it suitable for a fair child.

Yoko: Determined woman. In Japanese philosophy, Yo and In divide into heaven and earth when an egg splits. A name made famous in the West by Yoko Ono, who married Beatle John Lennon.

Yvonne: God is merciful. This French female form of Evan, the Welsh form of John, came to Britain this century and was a top favourite girl's name in the 1970s. Other forms: Evonne, Yvette.

Zara: Dawn. This form of Sarah was given a boost when Princess Anne named her daughter Zara Anne Elizabeth in 1981.

Zita: Seeker. The French saint is patroness of domestic servants. In Spain, the name means little rose. Other form: Zeta.

Zoe: Life-giving. This Greek form of Eve has been quite popular ever since the mid-19th century.

BOYS

Abraham: Eternal father of the multitudes. The name of first patriarch and father of the Hebrews was originally Abram, the favoured British form until after the Reformation.

Adam: Red earth. A biblical name given to the first man, the source of mankind. Restricted to the north of England until the Reformation, when Old Testament names became fashionable.

Adrian: Dark riches. The form Hadrian was adopted when the Roman emperor visited Britain. Adrian came later, popularised in the 12th century by the only English pope, Adrian IV.

Aidan: Little fiery one. A name found mostly in the north of England, probably because the Irish saint of that name founded a monastery at Lindisfarne in Northumbria.

Aiken: Made of oak. Old English name that has a second meaning in the north – little Adam, implying that the baby is the image of his father.

Alan: Peaceful harmony. The Celtic name may also have a Gaelic origin, meaning handsome, rock-solid. Introduced to Britain as Alain by the Normans and popular ever since, especially in Scotland. Other forms: Allan, Allen, Alun.

Alastair: Man's defender. Together with Alistair, the most popular English form of the Scottish Gaelic name Alasdair, which comes from Alexander.

Albert: Illustrious, noble. The German name, originally Adalbert, became highly fashionable when Queen Victoria married the German prince Albert in 1840. Other forms: Aubert, Bert, Bertie, Halbert.

Alexander: Man's defender. One of the oldest recorded names, kept popular through saints and kings, including Alexander the Great. Other forms: Alex, Alick, Alistair, Alix, Cassius, Sanders.

Alfred: Wise advice. Alfred the Great (849–99), the King of Wessex, kept the name popular until Tudor times, and it was revived again in the last century.

Algernon: With a moustache. A French name, allegedly created in the 11th century as a nickname of Eustace, Count of Boulogne, whose father was also named Eustace.

Alphonse: Ready for battle. Originally a German name, adopted in Spain and made famous by the astronomer Alphonsine the Wise. Other forms: Alfie, Alfons.

Alvin: Wise friend. An Old English name, popular now in the US.

Amadeus: Lovable. A name recently boosted by the film *Amadeus*, about the Austrian child prodigy and composer, Wolfgang Amadeus Mozart (1756–91).

Ambrose: Food of life, immortality. The 4th-century saint did less to popularise this name in Britain than Ambrosius Aurelianus, a real person upon whom the legendary King Arthur is perhaps based.

Amery: Hard-working in power. Originally a German name, Almeric, it was introduced to Britain by the Normans.

Amos: Troubled, worried. A biblical name popular with the Puritans because of its meaning.

Anatole: Rising sun. This is the Greek name for the main part of Turkey, and a meeting place for traders between the East and West in ancient times.

Andrew: Manly. Relics of the fisherman who became one of Christ's disciples were carried to Scotland where he became the country's patron saint. Consistently popular in Britain. Other forms: Anderson, Andie, Andreas, Andy, Drew.

Aneurin: Honour. This is either the Welsh form of Honour or an entirely Welsh name meaning pure gold. The politician Aneurin Bevan helped set up the National Health Service after World War II. Other forms: Aneirin, Nye.

Angus: Unique choice. A Scottish name, from Aonghus, rarely found elsewhere. Aonghus Turimleach, the legendary invader of Scotland, gave his name to the people and the breed of cattle.

Anthony: Flourishing. A popular Roman name, given to several emperors and to Mark Antony, Cleopatra's lover. The

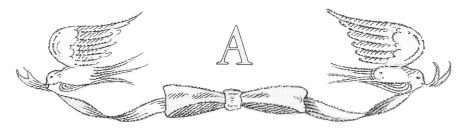

scholar Antony of Padua became the patron saint of lost property. Other forms: Anton, Antony, Tony.

Archibald: Extremely bold. Favoured by the Scottish Campbell and Douglas clans and boosted when their king, James VI, became James I of England, bringing his jester Archie Armstrong to London.

Arnold: Eagle power. An old name introduced by the Normans as Arnaud and later revived by the Victorians.

Arthur: Stone, rock. The name may also mean bear and may refer to the Norse god of war, Thor. The medieval and later Victorian obsession with the King Arthur legend kept the name in vogue. Queen Victoria called her son Arthur in honour of the Duke of Wellington, his godfather.

Ashley: Ash trees. A surname first adopted to honour the social reformer Lord Ashley, Earl of Shaftesbury.

Aubrey: Clever ruler. Derived from the Old German name Alberich and introduced to Britain in its French form, Auberi, by the Norman de Vere family who became Earls of Oxford.

Augustus: Worthy of honour. This esteemed title was awarded by the first Roman Emperor, Octavius Caesar, to himself. Later adopted by the German royal family whose descendants, the Hanoverian kings, brought it to Britain. Other forms: Augustine, Austin, Gus.

Austin: Worthy of honour. The French form of Augustus, brought to Britain by the Normans. Other form: Austen.

Baldwin: Bold friend. A German name that arrived from Flanders in the Middle Ages and also acquired a Welsh form, Maldwyn.

Barclay: *See* Berkeley.

Barnaby: Son of exhortation. A name implying the child is an answer to prayers. Popularised last century by the good-natured hero of Charles Dickens' *Barnaby Rudge* (1841). Other forms: Barnabas, Barnie.

Barnum: Barley store. A name made popular by the American pioneer of the Victorian circus, Phineas Taylor Barnum.

Baron: Warrior. The ancient feudal title for a king's tenant is now the lowest rank of British nobility, as well as a first name.

Barry: Spear. An old Celtic name that is still popular throughout Britain today, especially in Ireland. Other forms: Barnard, Barrie, Barrymore.

Bartholomew: Son of Talmai. The name of the Apostle-Saint was introduced by the Normans, since when 165 English churches have been dedicated to him. Further popularised by Henry I's court jester who founded St Bartholomew's hospital in London after recovering from an illness.

Basil: Kindly. St Basil the Great, Bishop of Caesarea, inspired Crusaders to bring the name home. More recently, the actor Basil Rathbone starred in a series of Sherlock Holmes films.

Beau: Handsome, beautiful. The French word was made popular by the fashionable dandy George Bryan Brummell (1778–1840), nicknamed Beau.

Beaumont: Beautiful mountain. This French place name became an English surname, then a popular Victorian first name.

Ben: Peak, mountain. The Gaelic word, used to describe Scottish mountains such as Ben Nevis, also means son in Hebrew. It is a form of Benedict and Benjamin.

Benedict: Blessed. The name has remained popular through two saints, Saint Benedict, the father of Western monasticism and St Benedict Biscop who founded monasteries at Wearmouth and Jarrow in the north of England. Other forms: Ben, Benett, Bennet, Benny.

Benjamin: Son of my right hand. A biblical name, given by Jacob to his favourite son. A popular Jewish name in Britain, given to the politician and novelist Benjamin Disraeli (1804–81) who converted to Christianity. Other forms: Ben, Benji, Benno.

Bentley: Field of coarse grass. A place name that was adopted as a first name in the last century, acquiring motor racing associations when W. O. Bentley's cars won the Le Mans race in the 1920s.

Berkeley: Birch wood. Another place name that became a first name and is found in Scotland as Barclay.

Bernard: Bearlike braveness. A Norman favourite, revived by the Victorians and popular in the 1920s. St Bernard is the patron saint of mountaineers. Other forms: Barnadin, Barny, Bernhard, Bjorn.

Bertrand: Bright shield, bright raven. The raven was the sacred bird of the Norse god Odin. Popular last century, when the Nobel prize-winning philosopher and pacifist Bertrand Russell (1872–1970) was born. Other forms: Bert, Bertram.

Bevis: Beautiful son. A French name brought over by the Normans, to be revived by the hero of Richard Jefferies' bestseller, *Bevis: The Story of a Boy* (1882). In Wales, it is the patronymic of Evan.

Blair: Flat land. The Scottish place name is a Celtic word implying a suitable place for a battle. Recently adopted as a first name.

Blake: Shining white. A surname recently adopted as a first name, as for Blake Edwards who wrote and directed the film *The Pink Panther* (1963).

Blaze: Flaming fire. A name implying dynamism and energy. The healing miracles of St Blaise have made him the patron saint of throat diseases.

Boris: To protect. A rare Russian import, boosted by the hero of Mussorgsky's opera *Boris Godunov* (1874), and chosen by William Pratt for his stage name, Boris Karloff (1887–1969).

Bradley: Broad clearing. The English place name was chosen by Charles Dickens for the passionate Bradley Headstone in *Our Mutual Friend* (1864–5). Other forms: Brad, Braden, Brady, Broderick.

Brendan: Stinking hair. St Brendan the Voyager, after whom the mountain in County Kerry is named, and Brennan of the Moor, the Irish Robin Hood, have kept this a firm Irish favourite. Other forms: Brandon, Brendon.

Brett: From Brittany. Breton was the Celtic word for the people of north-west France and their form of the Celtic language. Other form: Briton.

Brian: Hill. An Irish name popularised by the medieval king, Brian Boru, who drove the Norse armies out of Ireland in 1014. Also popular in Brittany, it was brought to Britain by the Normans. Other forms: Briant, Briar, Brien, Bryan, Bryon.

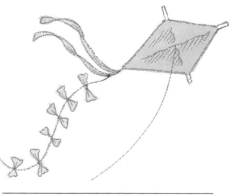

B-C

Brice: Son of the powerful ruler. The name of a 5th-century French saint much-loved in medieval Britain, especially Scotland.

Brindley: Burning wood. The place name, associated with a woodland clearing and also with the reddish-brown colour of wood, was used as a first name from late last century, but is uncommon now.

Brock: Badger. The Old English surname turned first name is also the traditional name for a badger in folk and children's stories, as Bruno is for bear.

Brook: Reward, pleasure. An Old English word adopted as a surname before it became a first name for both sexes.

Bruce: Copse, small wood. The French name Brieuse was brought to Britain by the Normans. Robert the Bruce, who seized the Scottish crown in 1306 and won Scotland's independence from England at the battle of Bannockburn in 1314, stimulated its use as a first name there.

Bruno: Brown, bear-like. A German name which is also the folk name for a bear, as Brock is for badger. Other forms: Brewis, Bronson, Browse.

Brutus: Heavy, unreasonable. The name of the Roman soldier and statesman who helped assassinate Julius Caesar, and was immortalised in Shakespeare's *Julius Caesar*.

Cameron: Bent nose. A Scottish clan name adopted as a first name and possibly encouraged by the 17th-century preacher Richard Cameron.

Campbell: Curved mouth. Like Cameron, a Celtic word that became a Scottish clan name and later a favourite Scottish first name.

Caradoc: Friendly. This popular Welsh name, from Caradawg, honours their 1st-century hero who repelled the Romans and after whom Cardigan is named. The Irish form is Carthac.

Carl: Free man, farmer. This German form of Charles has become popular in Britain and the US this century. Other forms: Karl, Karle.

Cary: *See* Charles.

Casey: Watchful, brave. An Irish name given to both sexes, and promoted by the heroism of train engineer Casey Jones (1864–1900), who saved many lives after the Cannon Ball Express accident.

Casper: Imperial, precious. Casper, Melchior and Balthasar were the Three Wise Men who brought gifts to the baby Jesus. The English form of this German name is Jasper.

Cassius: Man's defender. A Roman form of the Greek name; recently promoted by the American heavyweight boxer Cassius Marcellus Clay, who was named after the anti-slavery leader Cassius Clay (1810–1903). Also a form of Alexander.

Cecil: Blind. The name of the son of Vulcan, the Roman god of fire and craftsmanship, was at first given to both sexes in the Middle Ages, then revived for boys in the last century. Other forms: Cecile, Ces.

Cedric: Generous, friendly. Name of the legendary founder of Wessex and father of the British royal line, made popular by Sir Walter Scott's *Ivanhoe* (1819), and Frances Hodgson Burnett's *Little Lord Fauntleroy* (1886).

Chad: Fighter. The name of the 7th-century British saint Ceadda, noted for his humility, was revived last century.

Charles: Free man, farmer. Emperor Charles the Great (742–814), known as Charlemagne, was the founder of the Holy Roman Empire. In Britain, two Stuart kings and now the Prince of Wales, Charles Philip Arthur George, have kept it in fashion. Carl is the German form, Carol the French. Other forms: Carel, Carlie, Carlton, Carlyle, Cary, Chad, Charlie, Chas, Chick, Chuck, Karel.

Chester: Fortified castle or town. This place name has become more popular as a first name in the US than in Britain.

Christian: Anointed. A name promoted by Christian, the hero of John Bunyan's *Pilgrim's Progress* (1678–84). Recently revived, although still not as common as Christopher. Other forms: Christien, Krispin, Kristian.

Christopher: One who carries Christ. The legendary St Christopher, who carried the baby Jesus across a ford. Now the patron saint of all travellers, including motorists, familiar from countless pictures and models. Other forms: Chip, Chris, Christoph, Gilchrist, Kristofer.

Chuck: Free man, farmer. A popular American form of Charles.

Clarence: Shining brightly. The dukes of Clarence were named after the Suffolk town Clare, which was itself named after the Norman family de Clare, who also gave their name to County Clare in Ireland. Other forms: Claron, Sinclair.

Clark: Inheritance. The original name for the church scholars who were the only people who could read and write. Recently popularised by the actor Clark Gable (1901–60).

Claudius: Lame. The Roman emperor and historian, who walked with a limp, encouraged the name's use in Roman Britain, to be revived by the Tudors in its French form, Claude. Other forms: Claudian, Claudio, Claus.

Claus: *See* Claudius, Nicholas.

Clayton: Clay town. The place name, referring to local clay-pits or clay-beds, became a popular first name last century.

Clement: Gentle. A name made popular first by 14 popes, and more recently by the British Labour Prime Minister Clement Attlee (1883–1967). Other forms: Clem, Clemens.

Clinton: Hilltop town. A medieval place name and first name whose form Clint has more recently become popular due to the American film star Clint Eastwood.

Clive: Cliff, steep hill. A name chosen in the 18th and 19th centuries to honour the British soldier-statesman Robert Clive (1725–74), known as Clive of India. The old English form Cliff has become a more modern favourite through the pop singer Cliff Richard. Other forms: Clifford, Clifton.

Cole: Coal. A name derived from various mining place names, it has remained popular this century through the American songwriter, Cole Porter (1891–1964). Other forms: Colier, Collis, Colvin.

Colin: The people's triumph. This French short form of Nicholas has another meaning in Scotland and Ireland where it comes from the Celtic name Cailean meaning 'youth'. Other form: Colan.

Colwyn: Hazel copse. This form of the Welsh name, Collwyn, has been used in that country since medieval times.

Conan: High. Although the name of a 7th-century Irish chieftain, this name is primarily remembered through the Irish writer Sir Arthur Conan Doyle (1859–1930), who created the character Sherlock Holmes.

Connor: Lofty aims. A favourite Irish name, made popular by many heroes in Irish legend.

Conrad: Wise adviser. A German name that arrived in Britain in the Middle Ages, to be revived last century. It is the first name of hotel owner Conrad Hilton. Other forms: Conroy, Kurt.

Constantine: Steadfast, loyal. The Roman emperor Constantine the Great (*c*.280–337), a Christian convert and founder of Constantinople (now Istanbul), became ruler of the Western and Eastern Roman empires, ensuring the name's popularity with Christians and kings. Other forms: Connie, Constans, Costain.

Cosmo: Harmony, universe. A Greek name adopted by the powerful Medici family of Florence, it was introduced to Scotland by the 2nd Duke of Gordon who gave it to his son. Other form: Cosimo.

Craig: Of the rocks. A Welsh surname adopted as a first name in the 1940s and still popular today.

Crispin: Curled, curly-head. The 3rd-century shoemakers Crispin and Crispian are now patron saints of that trade. Both names were popular in the Middle Ages, but are less so now.

Cyril: Lord-like. First used during the Reformation, possibly in honour of the missionary and intellectual St Cyril. Revived in the 1930s. Other forms: Cy, Cyriack, Cyrill.

Dale: Valley. A place name adopted last century for both sexes but now confined to boys. Other forms: Dallas, Dalton, Dayle.

Damian: Divine power. The Greek tale of Damon offering to be executed in place of his friend gave the name its associations with loyal friendship. The American writer Damon Runyon (1884–1946), of *Guys and Dolls* fame, gave the name a boost this century.

Daniel: God is my judge. A popular biblical name in remembrance of the prophet whose faith saved him in the lion's den. Increasingly fashionable since the 1950s. Other forms: Dan, Danny, Danyele.

Darrell: Special, beloved. This surname turned first name has been fashionable since the 1940s, helped by film producer Darryl Zanuck who founded Twentieth Century Fox. Other forms: Darel, Darol, Darryl.

Darren: An Irish name that became popular in the 1960s, together with similar sounding names such as Sharon and Karen. Other forms: Daren, Daron, Darran, Darrin, Daryn.

David: Loved by God. A consistently popular name, helped by various heroes. The biblical King David was soldier, poet and musician; the patron saint of Wales was a 7th-century teetotaller; and the Scottish saint was a pious king. It has stayed in the top 10 since the 1950s. Other forms: Dafyd, Davey, Davis, Davy, Dawes, Dewi, Taffy.

Dean: Leader of 10 people. The Greek word came to mean a church officer. Only gained popularity as a first name this century, helped by the American singer Dean Martin, whose real name was Dino Crocetti. Other form: Dino.

Dennis: God of the Nysa. An anglicised form of the French name Denys, from the Greek god of wine and pleasure, Dionysus. Fashionable early this century, when the actor Dennis Price was born. Other forms: Denis, Denys, Denzel.

Denzil: The Cornish place name became a first name in Cornwall before spreading to other parts of Britain. Other forms: Denzel, Denzyl.

Derek: People's ruler. A popular medieval name, revived this century, to reach its height of popularity in the 1930s.

Dermot: Free from jealousy. The modern form of the old Irish name Diarmit is still popular in Ireland. Other forms: Dermott, Diarmid.

Desmond: Man from South Munster. An Irish surname taken up as a first name in the 18th century before crossing to mainland Britain.

Dominic: God's servant, God's day. Name of the Spanish saint who founded the Dominican Order in 1216, it was originally only given to children born on a Sunday. After the Reformation it was confined to Catholics, but now it is in general use. Other forms: Dom, Domenic, Dominique, Don.

Donald: World ruler. A Gaelic word that became a Scottish clan name, then a Scottish first name and that of the first Scottish Christian king. Other forms: Donahue, Donal, Donovan.

Dougal: Dark stranger. A Celtic name used by Irishmen to describe Englishmen, just as its original form Dugald described the Danes. A favourite in the Scottish Highlands.

Douglas: Dark water. A Scottish clan name that refers to the Isle of Man's capital, built where two streams meet. A favourite in Scotland for both sexes until it was confined to boys this century.

Drake: Serpent, dragon. From the Greek, a snake name associated with the mythology of many countries, and symbolising wisdom and immortality.

Drew: Manly. This Scottish short form of Andrew gained full independence in the 1960s.

Dudley: Dudo's meadow. Dudley Castle was supposedly built by the Saxon Prince Dodo. A name made popular by the British actor and pianist Dudley Moore.

Duff: Dove. The name symbolising peace and love was given a boost this century by Duff Cooper, politician and husband of the society beauty Lady Diana Cooper.

Duke: Leader, guide. This Latin name may also be a short form of the Irish name Marmaduke. Recently, it was the nickname for both the actor John Wayne and jazz musician Duke Ellington.

Duncan: Dark warrior. The name of the Scottish king murdered by his cousin and featured in Shakespeare's *Macbeth*, has remained most popular in Scotland.

D-E

Dunstan: Stony hill, stone-brown colour. The 10th-century English saint who was Archbishop of Canterbury made up the coronation rite still used by the British monarchy. Another form of the name was recently revived through the American actor Dustin Hoffman. Other forms: Dunn, Dusty.

Dwight: God of the Nysa. Like Dennis, this British form of the French name Diot derives from Dionysus. More popular in the US, where it honours President Dwight David Eisenhower (1890–1971), known as Ike.

Dylan: Sea. The Welsh name of the legendary hero born of a sea-god was given to the poet Dylan Marlais Thomas (1914–53).

Eamon: Fortunate protector. This Irish form of Edmund was the name of the Irish President Eamon de Valera (1882–1975). The television presenter Eamonn Andrews has made it better known in England.

Earl: Warrior chief. Like Duke, a name adopted from a title of rank in the 17th century. More popular in the US, it is the name of the author, Erle Stanley Gardner (1889–1970), who created Perry Mason.

Edgar: Lucky spear. The first recognised king of England was Edgar the Peaceful, grandson of Alfred the Great. The hero of Sir Walter Scott's romance *The Bride of Lammermoor* (1819) stimulated its revival last century. Other form: Eadgar.

Edmund: Fortunate protector. Old English name that retained its popularity through three early kings and one saint. The Irish form is Eamon; the French, Edmond.

Edward: Fortunate protector. A royal name, given to Edward the Elder, the king and saint, Edward the Confessor, and eight kings after the Norman Conquest. Also the name of the Queen's youngest son. Other forms: Eddie, Edison, Eduard, Ned, Ted, Teddy.

Edwin: Lucky friend. Edinburgh, capital city of Scotland, is possibly named after the 7th-century Christian king of Northumbria, and the name is still popular in Scotland and the north.

Eliot: High. A Scottish form of Eli, which was a popular biblical name during the Reformation, and today in the US. Other forms: Eliott, Elliott.

Elton: Ella's place. A place name adopted late last century and recently boosted by the singer Elton John (real name, Reginald), who chose it in honour of the saxophonist Elton Dean.

Elvis: Clever friend. An American name possibly adapted from Elvin, or from the trade name for cars, Alvis. Made fashionable in Britain by the rock-and-roll star Elvis Aaron Presley (1935–77).

Emanuel: God is here. The biblical name for Christ is a popular Jewish name. Among non-Jews it was found in Cornwall before spreading into general use last century. Other forms: Emmanuel, Imanuel, Manny, Manuel.

Emery: Power. The anglicised form of the German name Emmerich was given to both sexes until confined to boys in the last century.

Enoch: Dedicated. The name of Cain's son in the Bible, it was favoured by the Puritans and boosted by Tennyson's tragic poem *Enoch Arden* (1864). It is now found mostly in the north and Midlands, where the politician Enoch Powell was born.

Eric: Consistent ruler. The name of the Norse chieftain became fashionable in Britain with Sir Henry Rider Haggard's romance *Eric Brighteyes* (1891).

Ernest: Intensely determined. A German aristocratic name brought to Britain by the Hanoverian kings, later revived by Oscar Wilde in his successful play *The Importance of Being Earnest* (1895).

Errol: Warrior chief. This German form of Earl may also be derived from a Scottish place name. The film actor Errol Flynn (1909–59), who came from Northern Ireland, made the name popular in Britain and the US.

Erskine: Cliff high. The Scottish place name, adopted as a first name in the last century, gained recognition through the writer Erskine Childers (1870–1922), author of *The Riddle of the Sands*.

Eugene: Well-born, fortunate. A popular name in the last century inspired by Napoleon's wife – the female form is Eugénie. Mostly given to boys now, it is sometimes shortened to Gene. Other forms: Owen.

Eustace: Bountiful, fruitful. A name boosted by the medieval legend of St Eustace, who was converted to Christianity when he saw a vision of the cross. Other forms: Eustis, Stacy.

Evelyn: Hazelnut. Associated with the Celtic fruit of wisdom. Introduced by the Normans as a girl's name, then extended to boys in the 17th century. The novelist Evelyn Waugh (1903–66) gave it recognition this century.

Falkner: Falcon. A name adapted from falconer; someone who trains the highly-valued hunting birds.

Felix: Good fortune. Popular in the Middle Ages – more than 60 saints bore the name. Still used today, but less common than the female form, Felicia.

Ferdinand: Wild, headstrong. A royal name found in medieval Europe, it was carried to Britain by the Normans and taken up mainly in the Midlands. Shakespeare used it for the young hero in *The Tempest*.

Fergus: Best choice. A form of the Celtic name Feargus, one of the legendary Irish founders of Scotland, and still found mainly in those two countries.

Finn: Fair, white. The legendary Irish hero who defended Ireland with his supernatural powers, and St Finnian, the founder of Irish monasticism, make this a popular name in Ireland.

Forbes: Grazing grass, field. A Scottish place name adopted as a first name, and chosen mainly in Scotland.

Francis: Independent. A name kept popular by saints and royals, notably St Francis of Assisi, the patron saint of ecology. Particularly popular in Britain under the Tudors, then out of favour until the early 19th century. Other forms: Frank, Franklin.

Fraser: Charcoal maker. A surname adopted as a first name this century, especially in Scotland.

Frederick: Peaceful ruler. Despite its German meaning, most of the royal Fredericks have been war-loving, including Frederick the Great (1712–86), King of Prussia. He encouraged the Hanoverians to introduce the name to Britain, where it became a favourite in the 19th century. Other forms: Eric, Fred, Freddie, Fritz, Ricky.

Gabriel: God's hero. The name of the archangel who told Mary that she would give birth to Jesus is found mostly in Ireland. Other forms: Gabby, Gabryel.

Gareth: Gentle. A Welsh name revived by Victorian medievalists after Tennyson recounted the Arthurian romance of Gareth and Lynette in his epic poem *Idylls of the King* (1859). A favourite 1980s name. Other forms: Garth, Gary.

Garfield: Field of spears. A surname adopted as a first name and boosted by the West Indian cricketer Sir Garfield St Auburn Sobers, known as Gary.

Gary: A short form of Gerald, Gareth and Garfield, made popular in this century by the American actor Gary Cooper (1901–61), who changed his name from Frank.

Gavin: White hawk. This Scottish form of the medieval Welsh name Gawain spread from Scotland in the 1950s to become a favourite British name. Other forms: Gavan, Gawen, Walwyn.

Geoffrey: Peace. The name has several possible origins, all connected with peace. Introduced by the Normans and made famous by the father of English poetry, Geoffrey Chaucer (1342–1400). Consistently popular since the last century. Other forms: Geoff, Godfrey, Jeff, Jefferson, Jeffrey.

George: Farmer. The legendary Roman martyr who slew the dragon and became patron saint of England. A popular name for English kings since the 18th century. Other forms: Georgie, Igor, Jorge, Yuri.

Geraint: Old. This medieval Welsh name derives from Gerontius. The Victorian revival of the Arthurian legend of Geraint and Enid promoted the name which was given to the Welsh singer Sir Geraint Llewellyn Evans.

Gerald: Spear rule, warrior rule. A French name introduced by the Normans and revived in the 1950s. Another form, Gerard, came via Ireland and Wales. Other forms: Garcia, Gary, Gerry, Gervase, Jerrard, Jerry.

Gideon: He cut down. The hard-working biblical judge and warrior was the inspiration of the Gideons, a Christian organisation which places Bibles in hotel and hospital rooms.

Giles: Kid goat. Originally a name for both sexes, it was inspired by St Giles, the patron saint of cripples and the poor.

Glyn: Small valley. A Celtic name popular in Scotland even before Sir Walter Scott's novels spread it further. The form Glen is more popular in Canada and the US.

Godfrey: *See* Geoffrey.

Gordon: Wooded dell. Like Clive, a surname used to honour a hero, this time General Gordon of the ancient Scottish clan, who was killed in 1885 while defending Khartoum.

Graham: Granta's place. A place name adopted by a Scottish clan. Already a first

name by medieval times, it spread into the rest of Britain in the 19th century. Other forms: Graeme, Grahame.

Granger: Grainstore. Once a name for a farm labourer, it was adopted as a first name recently and became popular with the help of the actor Stewart Granger.

Grant: Tall or promise. Although long popular in Scotland, recent fashion in Britain may be due to its use in the US.

Gray: Grey. The colour may have once referred to grey hair or to cloaks of the Franciscan and Cistercian monks, known as the Greyfriars. Other forms: Grey, Greyson.

Gregory: Watchful. A Greek name brought to England by a missionary of Gregory the Great (540–604). Recently regained popularity through the American actor Gregory Peck. Other forms: Greg, Gregg, Gregor, Grig.

Guy: Lively. St Guy is patron saint of comedians and dancers. The name was popular in Britain until Guy Fawkes tried to blow up Parliament in 1605; but it was later revived by Sir Walter Scott's novel *Guy Mannering* (1815).

Haddon: Heathland. An unusual Scottish name, sometimes found as Hadley.

Hamish: Supplanter. The anglicised form of Sheumais and Seumas – Gaelic forms of James – is rarely found outside Scotland.

Hans: God's mercy. The German and Dutch short form for Johannes, from John, made famous by Hans Christian Andersen who published his first collection of fairy tales in 1835.

Harold: Army leader. A name introduced to England by Harold I and his son, Harold II, who was killed at the Battle of Hastings in 1066. Revived in the 19th century and borne by two recent Prime Ministers, Harold Macmillan (1894–1986) and Harold Wilson.

Harvey: Suitable for battle. A Norman introduction from Brittany, where the blind wandering minstrel St Harvey was popular.

Hayden: Pastureland. A surname turned first name, perhaps for its pleasant associations with the verdant summer countryside.

Hector: Anchor. In England, the name of the Trojan hero who led the fight against the Greeks for 10 years. In Scotland, where it is more popular, it is a form of the Gaelic name Eachdoin, meaning horse lord.

Hedley: Meadow for sheep. In Old English dialect, a heder was a young male

sheep. A place name adopted as a first name last century.

Henry: Ruler of the house. An old name that has remained in fashion for centuries. Given to eight kings of England, it was also chosen for the Prince of Wales's second son, Henry Charles Albert David, known as Harry. Other forms: Barry, Darris, Hadrick, Hal, Hank, Harrison, Hendrick, Henri, Heriot.

Herbert: Illustrious fighter. A Norman name, revived in the 19th century when the author Herbert George Wells (1866–1946) and the actor-producer Herbert Beerbohm Tree (1853–1917) were born. Other forms: Bert, Bertie, Heber, Herbie.

Herman: Soldier. A German name introduced by the Normans and revived last century, it has always been an unusual choice in Britain.

Hilary: Cheerful. A name for both sexes, it was introduced by the Puritans to honour St Hilary of Arles. Other forms: Hilaire, Hillary, Hilliard.

Horace: Time, hour. A popular Roman name, revived in the 18th century in admiration of the writer and wit Horace Walpole (1717–97), and the admiral Horatio Nelson (1758–1805).

Howard: Guardian of hogs or sheep. A name long popular in the US, where it was given to the millionaire, magnate and recluse Howard Hughes (1905–78), but only more recently popular in Britain.

Howell: Eminent. This anglicised form of the Welsh name Hywel may also come from the English place name meaning 'hill for swine'. Other forms: Hoel, Howel.

Hugh: Outstanding in mind and spirit. An old name, recently popularised by Hugh Gaitskell, leader of the Labour Party (1955–63). The Welsh forms are Huw and Hew. Other forms: Hubert, Hughie, Hugo.

Humphrey: Peace. The anglicised form of the Norman name Onfroi was popular with the Hanoverians, and came back into fashion this century with the actor Humphrey Bogart (1899–1957) and the jazz musician Humphrey Lyttelton.

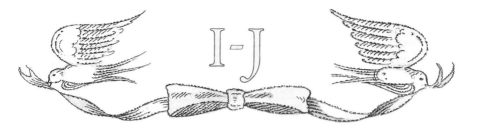

Ian: God's mercy. This Scottish form of John only became popular last century, to become a British top favourite in the 1960s. Other forms: Iain, Ion.

Irving: Fair, handsome. Another Scottish name to emerge last century, made popular by the Russian-born American song-writer Irving Berlin, whose real name was Israel Baline.

Ivan: The Russian form of John gained favour last century with other Russian imports, such as Olga and Sonia. Other forms: Evon, Ivo.

Ivor: Lord. A form of the Welsh name Ifor, popularised by the actor-manager and composer David Ivor Novello (1893–1951).

Jack: God's mercy. This form of John arrived from the Low Countries in the Middle Ages and was soon popular enough to be used in stories and rhymes such as Jack and the Beanstalk, Jack and Jill, Jack Sprat.

Jacob: Supplanter. In the Bible, the twin brother of Esau who gained both shares of the inheritance and became the founding father of the tribes of Israel. A favourite Jewish name, given to the sculptor Sir Jacob Epstein (1880–1959). Other forms: Cobb, Jackson, Jacques, Jago, Jake, James.

Jake: A form of Jacob that has gained full independence since the 1960s, when it was at its most fashionable.

James: Supplanter. The English form of Jacob was the name of two of Christ's Apostles, two British kings and six Scottish kings. Of names announced in *The Times* newspaper, James has been the most popular for 23 years. Hamish is the Scottish Highlands form; Seamus and its variants are the Irish. Other forms: Diego, Hamish, Jaimie, Jamie, Jas, Jay, Jim, Jimmy.

Jamie: Supplanter. This form of James has won such popularity that it has now become one of the top 40 British favourites, quite independently from James.

Janus: Gateway. This unusual name comes from first month, January, named after Janus who was the double-faced Roman god of endings and beginnings.

Jason: God is my saviour. This form of Joshua was the name of the mythological Greek hero who found the Golden Fleece. Its popularity today has been helped by the actor Jason Robards.

Jaspar: Imperial, precious. This is the English form of the German name Casper. Other forms: Gasper, Jasper.

Jay: To rejoice. From the Roman name Gaius, the bird may have been so named for its chirping.

Jeffrey: *See* Geoffrey.

Jeremy: God is on high. The English form of Jeremiah, the Old Testament prophet. Popular in the 18th century when philosopher Jeremy Bentham (1748–1832) advocated striving for the greatest happiness for the greatest number of people, it has had a recent revival. Other forms: Gerry, Jerry.

Jerome: Sacred. St Jerome (304–84), one of the great church scholars, stimulated the name's popularity in medieval times. More recently Jerome K. Jerome was author of *Three Men in a Boat* (1889).

Jesse: God beholds. In the Bible, Jesse was the father of King David. Enjoyed some popularity in the last century through the American outlaw hero Jesse

James (1847–82). Other form: Jess.

Jethro: Abundance. A biblical name and that of the English inventor and agriculturalist Jethro Tull (1674–1741). Other forms: Jeth, Jett.

Jocelin: Of the Goths. This word for the German people was introduced by the Normans. Other forms: Jocelyn, Joclyn, Joscelyn, Joss, Josslyn.

Joel: God's willingness. A biblical name first taken up by the Puritans.

John: God's mercy. The most popular boys' name since the 17th century, to the extent that 'John Bull' has become the personification of England in political satire. Ian is the Scottish form, Sean the Irish, Ivan the Russian, Hans the Dutch,

Yves the French. Other forms: Evan, Ewan, Haines, Jack, Jan, Jennings, Jock, Johnnie, Jon, Owen, St John, Yank.

Jolyon: *See* Julian.

Jonathan: God's gift. A name associated with the deep friendship of David and Jonathan in the Bible; further popularised by Jonathan Swift, author of *Gulliver's Travels* (1726).

Joseph: God multiplies. Two biblical figures – Jacob's favourite son and the Virgin Mary's husband – have kept the name in favour. Other forms: Giuseppe, Joe, Josko, Pepe.

Joshua: God is my saviour. An Old Testament name, popular after the Reformation. The painter Joshua Reynolds (1723–92) was the first President of the Royal Academy. Other forms: Jason, Jesus, Josh.

Jude: Praise. St Jude is patron saint of lost causes. The name was promoted by Thomas Hardy's novel *Jude the Obscure* (1895).

Julian: Soft-haired, or descended from Jove. A name derived from Julius but popularised by St Julian, patron saint of travellers, innkeepers and boatmen. Other forms: Jolin, Jolyon, Jules.

Justin: Righteous, just. The Christian martyr, not the Byzantine emperor, probably encouraged the name's popularity in medieval Britain. A name now in favour once more.

Keith: Wood. A Gaelic name that spread from Scotland in the last century to become a favourite in the 1950s.

Kelvin: Friend of ships. The name of a Scottish river, it gained favour throughout Britain in the 1920s.

Kenneth: Handsome. An exclusively Scottish name, honouring their 9th-century hero Kenneth McAlpine, until it became a British favourite in the 1950s. Other forms: Cinead, Kenny.

Kevin: Handsome at birth. This Irish name was popularised by St Kevin, who founded Glendalough monastery near Dublin. It became fashionable throughout Britain in the 1960s. Other forms: Coemgen, Kevan, Kevyn.

Kingsley: King's wood or meadow. A surname turned first name in the late 19th century, promoted today by the novelist Kingsley Amis.

Kirk: Church. The Old Norse word became a first name last century, and was made popular this century by the US actor Kirk Douglas whose real name is Yssur Danilovitch Demsky.

Lambert: Bright as the land. A popular name in the Middle Ages, honouring the Flemish saint; it has been revived recently.

Lance: Spear. A form of Lancelot, the dashing legendary knight whose affair with Queen Guinevere led to war with King Arthur. Revived by Victorian medievalists, especially in the north.

Laurence: Laurel. A saintly name – Shakespeare gave it to the kindly friar in *Romeo and Juliet* – and one that symbolises achievement. Popular this century, helped by the success of the actor Sir Laurence Olivier. Other forms: Larkin, Larry, Lars, Laurens, Laurie, Lorence, Lorens, Lorne.

Lee: Wood, clearing, meadow. A surname turned first name in the US, it came to Britain with the actors Lee J. Cobb and Lee Marvin and has become a 1980s favourite.

Len: *See* Leonard.

Leo: Lion. This was the popular form until the last century when Leon was also used. Other forms: Len, Lennie, Lionel, Llewellyn.

Leonard: Lion-hearted. The 5th-century hermit saint, patron of prisoners, and the Renaissance genius Leonardo da Vinci kept the name alive until it became fashionable this century. Other forms: Len, Lennard, Lennie, Lonnie.

Leslie: Low-lying meadow. A Scottish family name adopted for girls, then boys.

The actor Leslie Howard made it a great favourite in the 1940s and '50s, but Bob Hope abandoned it after he was nicknamed Hope Less.

Lewis: Glorious in war. This anglicised form of the French name Louis was chosen by Lewis Carroll, the creator of *Alice in Wonderland* (1865), whose real name was Charles Lutwidge Dodgson.

Lindsey: Linden tree. The family name of the Scottish Earls of Crawford was given to boys until the 1930s, since when it has been preferred for girls. Other forms: Lindsay, Linsey.

Lionel: Little lion. This form of Leo was encouraged this century by the actor Lionel Barrymore (1878–1954) and the composer Lionel Bart, who wrote the musical *Oliver* (1960).

Louis: Glorious in war. This French name, borne by French kings for 11 centuries, has again become popular through the jazz musician Louis Armstrong (1900–71). Other forms: Clovis, Elois, Lewis, Lou, Ludovicus, Ludwig, Luigi, Luis.

Lucien: Shining out. Derived from Lucius, this name has recently been boosted by the Italian tenor Luciano Pavarotti.

Luke: From Lucania. A name made lastingly popular by the physician and artist St Luke the Evangelist, patron saint of doctors and painters.

Luther: Famous people. A name honouring the German reformer and Bible translator Martin Luther (1483–1546); recently revived by the American clergyman and civil rights leader Martin Luther King (1929–68).

Magnus: Great, noble. A Scottish name imported from the Scandinavian royal family and now more widely used in Britain.

Malcolm: St Columba's servant. A Scottish royal name, held by Malcolm III (1031–93) who, with his queen Margaret, converted Scotland to Roman Catholicism. Popular in Britain since the 1930s.

Mark: Shining. The name, from the Roman god of war, Mars, was given to St Mark the Evangelist who made it a Christian favourite. Mark Twain, American author of *Tom Sawyer* (1876), chose it in preference to Samuel Langhorne Clemens. Other forms: Marc, Marcel, March, Marcus, Marion, Marius, Martin.

Martin: Shining. This French form of Mark, made popular by St Martin of Tours and Martin Luther (1483–1546), enjoyed a revival in the 19th century. Other forms: Martel, Martie, Martyn.

Matthew: God's gift. The name of one of Christ's disciples, it has remained consistently popular until the last century, to be keenly revived in the 1940s. Other forms: Mathias, Matias, Matt, Matthias, Mattie.

Maurice: Dark-skinned, Moorish. The Swiss saint's name was brought to Britain by the Normans, its use this century boosted by the French entertainer Maurice Chevalier (1888–1972). Other forms: Maur, Morrice, Morris.

Max: Greatest. A short form of Maximillian, Maxwell and Maxime, made more popular this century by the caricaturist Sir Max Beerbohm (1872–1956) and the singer Max Bygraves.

Maynard: Very strong. A German name known today through the economist John Maynard Keynes (1883–1946).

Melvin: Friendly meeting. Only in use since the last century the name may also be derived from the Scottish surname or the girl's name Malvina, invented by the poet James Macpherson.

Merlin: *See* Mervyn.

Mervyn: Sea hill. This English form of the Welsh name Myrddin derives from the name of the wizard who advised the legendary King Arthur. Other forms: Marlon, Merle, Merlin, Merlon.

M·N

Michael: Who can be like God? The patron saint of soldiers is God's archangel. A top favourite since medieval times, it was the name chosen for the Disney cartoon character Mickey Mouse. Other forms: Michel, Mick, Micky, Mike, Miles, Mitch, Mitchell.

Miles: Gentle, generous. A name popular in Ireland where it also absorbed the meaning 'servant of Mary'. Other forms: Milo, Myles.

Milton: Mill town. A first name taken from the surname, whose most famous holder was the poet John Milton (1608–74).

Morris: Dark-skinned, Moorish. A form of Maurice popular in the last century, when William Morris (1834–96) encouraged Victorian medievalism and founded the Arts and Crafts Movement.

Moses: Saved and saviour. Hidden among bulrushes as a baby to save his life, this biblical hero led the Israelites out of Egypt and received the Ten Commandments from God. A name always popular with Jewish families. Other forms: Moshe, Moss, Moy.

Murphy: Of the sea. This Celtic name is an Irish favourite, even though Murphy's Law states that if anything can go wrong, it will.

Murray: Sea. A Celtic name, traditionally favoured by Scottish families. Other forms: Moray, Murry.

Napoleon: New town. A name inspired by the brilliant military technician Napoleon Bonaparte (1769–1821), it has never become popular in Britain.

Nathaniel: God's gift. A biblical name that gained popularity after the Reformation, to be revived recently.

Neil: Champion. This Gaelic name, derived from Niul and Niall, spread from Scotland this century to become a British favourite in the 1950s, boosted by the American astronaut Neil Armstrong's moon walk in 1969. Other forms: Neal, Neall, Neill, Nelson, Nial, Niel.

Neville: New town. A French name popular under the Stuarts and revived in the last century when the Conservative politician Neville Chamberlain (1869–1940) was born.

Newton: New town. This English form of Neville was given by D. H. Lawrence to a jolly character in his novel *Sons and Lovers* (1913).

Nicholas: The people's triumph. The name of the patron saint of children, sailors, merchants and pawnbrokers is still a British favourite. Other forms: Claus, Colin, Klaus, Nic, Nick, Nickie, Nicky, Nico, Nicolas.

Nigel: Black. This popular form of the Roman name Nigellus may also be a derivative of either Daniel or Neil.

Noel: Birth, birthday. The French word for Christmas, formerly given to both

sexes, was popularised this century by the playwright and actor Noel Coward (1899–1973).

Norman: North. An Old English name referring to Norwegians, not Normans. Revived last century, especially in Scotland, it was the name of the Queen's dressmaker Sir Norman Hartnell (1901–79).

Ogden: Valley of oaks. Old English name promoted this century by the poet and humorist Ogden Nash (1902–71).

Oliver: Olive. The name for the ancient symbol of peace, firmly out of fashion after Oliver Cromwell, was revived in the 19th century when Charles Dickens wrote *Oliver Twist* (1838). Now a British favourite. Other forms: Nollie, Olivier.

Omar: Long life, most high. The name was introduced to Britain when the medieval Persian poet Omar Khayyam's *Ruba'iyat* was published in English in 1859. Although uncommon today, it has been given a boost by the film star Omar Sharif.

Orlando: *See* Roland.

Osbert: Shining god. A name originally confined to the north of England where Os had been the prefix of the Northumbrian rulers, but revived throughout Britain last century.

Oscar: God-spear. This Old English name was used by the Irish-born wit and writer Oscar Wilde (1854–1900), whose real name was Fingal O'Flahertie Wills, and given to Oscar Hammerstein (1895–1960) who with Richard Rodgers wrote *The Sound of Music* (1959).

Osmond: God's protection. A name made popular by St Osmund, who was William the Conqueror's Chancellor and Bishop of Salisbury, to be revived with other old names last century.

Oswald: God of the woods, God of power. Like Osbert, a popular Northumbrian name, revived last century when it was given to Oswald Ernald Mosley (1896–1980) who founded the British Union of Fascists in 1933.

Otis: Prosperous. A form of Otto that was adopted as a first name in the US to honour the patriot James Otis (1725–83), before being made famous in Britain by the singer Otis Redding.

Otto: Prosperous. A German royal name that has never been popular in Britain, it is best known here as the name of Germany's Iron Chancellor, Otto von Bismarck (1815–98).

Owen: Well-born, fortunate. A Welsh favourite since the 18th century, in recognition of the medieval hero Owen Glendower. Other forms: Bowen, Bowie, Ewan, Ewen, Owain.

Painton: Country town. A name introduced by the Normans but only used occasionally today.

Paris: The name of the romantic Greek hero whose elopement with Helen caused the Trojan War. Also a short form of Patrick.

Patrick: Aristocrat. The name of the patron saint of Ireland was thought too sacred to use until the 17th century, since when it has become a favourite there. Long popular in Scotland, from where it reached the rest of Britain. Other forms: Paddy, Padraig, Paris, Pat, Patrice, Pattison, Paxton, Peter, Peyton.

Paul: Small. Christ's Apostle, who chose the name in favour of Saul after his conversion, had more than 300 churches named after him, including St Paul's Cathedral in London. Popular in the 17th century, and again today.

Percival: Warrior of fire. A medieval French name, given to one of King Arthur's legendary knights, and revived by the Victorian medievalists. Less common today.

Peregrine: Traveller, pilgrim. An early Christian name popular under the Hanoverians, then revived in a short form with the fictional detective Perry Mason.

Peter: Rock. The leader of Christ's disciples was also the first pope which accounts for the name's popularity in Britain until the Reformation.

Its revival this century was due to J. M. Barrie's play *Peter Pan* (1904). Other forms: Parnell, Parry, Pete, Pier, Piers, Rockie.

Philip: Horse-loving. The name of one of Christ's disciples acquired royal character through Spanish and French kings but, like Peter, was ousted by the Protestants. Its current fashion is helped by Prince Philip, Duke of Edinburgh.

Piers: Rock. This French form of Peter was used in Britain before Peter itself, hence the hero of the medieval poem *Piers Plowman*. Regained popularity in the 1930s. Other forms: Peers, Pierre.

Prince: Chief. This Roman name adopted as a British surname was given to black American slaves. Only used as a first name this century, but still not widely.

Quentin: Fifth. The anglicised name of the Scottish saint, Quinctian, was revived by Sir Walter Scott in *Quentin Durward* (1823), and is gaining popularity again.

Raleigh: Deer's pasture. A name honouring Sir Walter Raleigh, a favourite of Queen Elizabeth I. The capital of North Carolina (USA) is named after him.

Ralph: Courageous adviser. A name popular since the Tudors but pronounced 'rafe' until early this century. *Ralph Roister Doister* is the first known English comedy, written by Nicholas Udall (1505–65), a headmaster of Eton School. Other forms: Ralf, Ralston, Randolph, Raoul.

Ramsay: Sheep's or raven's island. This ancient Scottish surname became a first name and was made better known by James Ramsay MacDonald (1866–1937), Britain's first Labour Prime Minister.

Randolph: Courageous protector. Popular as Randal in the Middle Ages, this name was given to the statesman Randolph Churchill (1849–95), Winston Churchill's father.

Raymond: Wise guardian. A name popular with crusaders, it was revived last century and became a favourite in the 1930s, helped by the actors Raymond Massey and Raymond Burr.

Rex: Leader. This male form of Regina only emerged as a first name late last century, and is usually a short form of Reginald, as for the actor Rex Harrison.

Rhys: Rashness, passion. A Welsh royal name, made popular in another form with Margaret Mitchell's hero Rhett in *Gone with the Wind* (1936). Other form: Reece.

Richard: Strong ruler. The name of three Plantagenet kings, it has remained popular ever since. This century, the politician Richard (Rab) Butler (1902–82) instigated free education for all, and the Welsh actor Richard Burton married Elizabeth Taylor twice. Other forms: Dick, Dickie, Hick, Hudd, Hudson, Richardson, Richie, Rick, Rocco.

Robert: Illustrious fame. Two legendary heroes – Robin Hood and Robin Goodfellow – made this form popular in Britain. Robert Peel (1788–1850), twice Conservative Prime Minister, founded the Metropolitan Police Force, who were nicknamed 'Bobbies' after him. Other forms: Bob, Bobby, Dobbs, Dobson, Hopkins, Nobbie, Robbie, Robertson.

Robin: *See* Robert.

Roderick: Famous ruler. A predominantly Scottish name, it comes from the Old German name Hrodric and the Gaelic Ruairidh, meaning red.

Rodney: Reed island. A first name adopted in the 18th century to honour the hero, Admiral George Brydges, Lord Rodney (1719–92), who took his title from the English village, Rodney Stoke.

Roger: Illustrious fighter. This Norman import became so popular in the Middle Ages that, as with Hick and Dick for Richard, it produced the nicknames Dodge and Hodge. Became popular again in the 1950s and has remained so.

Roland: Countrywide fame. The name of the most famous of Charlemagne's knights, and hero of medieval romances, reached the peak of its revival in the 1920s. The Italian form, Orlando, became popular in Britain later, perhaps helped by Shakespeare's *Twelfth Night*. Other forms: Orlando, Rolland, Rowland.

Rolf: Famous for bravery. The Normans introduced this form of the German name Hrodult, but it was revived in its full form, Rudolph, last century, to be promoted recently by the Russian dancer Rudolph Nureyev. The form Rolf has been made better known here in recent years by the Australian entertainer, Rolf Harris. Other forms: Rollo, Rudolf.

Ronald: Mightiness. The cousin of Charlemagne's son Roland made this another medieval favourite, to be revived by the Victorians together with Reynold and Reginald.

Rory: Red. This anglicised form of the Gaelic Ruairidh, meaning red, was confined to Scotland and Ireland until this century.

Ross: Peninsular. A Scottish place name adopted last century, and becoming more popular now. Also a short form of the Dutch name Roosevelt, field of roses, adopted in the US to honour Franklin Delano Roosevelt (1882–1945).

Rowan: Fair and slender. This anglicised form of the Welsh girl's name Rhonwen is used in Ireland as yet another form of the Gaelic Ruairidh, meaning red.

Roy: Red. Like Rory, an anglicised form of the Gaelic name Ruairidh, although often short for Roydon and Royston. Its popularity in the 1940s was helped by 'King of the Cowboys' actor Roy Rogers.

Rufus: Red. The Latin word was often used as a nickname for redheads and was given to King William II (1056–1100) – Rufus the Red.

Rupert: Illustrious fame. This German form of Robert came to Britain with Charles I's nephew Prince Rupert and may have gained favour in the 1920s through the popularity of the cartoon character Rupert Bear.

Russell: Red. This aristocratic surname, originally a French nickname like Rufus, was adopted as a first name last century to become a favourite in the 1950s. Other forms: Russ, Russel.

Ryan: Little king. A popular Irish name that only crossed to mainland Britain in the 1960s.

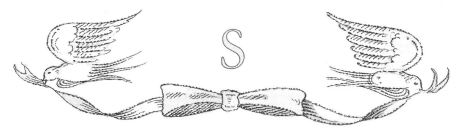

Samson: Sun. The name of the biblical judge and strongman was given to a popular Welsh saint. Revived after the Reformation, but not widely in use now.

Samuel: Heard. A name implying the answer to parents' prayers, it has remained popular since the Reformation, when it was chosen for its biblical reference to the prophet. Other forms: Sam, Sammy.

Saul: Asked for. A biblical name – the first king of Israel was Saul and it was the original name of the Apostle who became Paul when he converted; it is less common today than Paul.

Scott: The Old English name for the Gaelic-speaking people of Ireland who moved to Scotland. Popular only since the 1940s, particularly in the US, becoming a British favourite in the 1970s.

Seamus: Supplanter. This Irish form of James gained favour in mainland Britain in the 1950s. Other forms: Seumas, Seumus, Shamus.

Sean: *See* Shaun.

Sebastian: Venerable. The name of the Roman saint martyred with arrows was popular on the Continent. Imported by the Tudor playwrights, it has enjoyed a revival helped by the athlete Sebastian Coe. Other forms: Seb, Sebastien, Steb.

Selwyn: Close friend. An English name, but mostly found in Wales where it takes on the Welsh meaning, 'fair zeal'.

Serge: Servant. A French form of a Roman family name, used as Sergei for the two Russian composers Rachmaninoff and Prokofiev.

Seth: Appointed. The name of Adam and Eve's third son became popular under the Hanoverians and gained some favour in the 19th century with George Eliot's novel *Adam Bede* (1859).

Shaun: God's mercy. This Irish form of John came to mainland Britain as Sean in the 1920s and rose to popularity in the '60s when Sean Connery starred in the James Bond films. Now a favourite name.

Sherlock: Area of land. A name made popular in the last century by Sir Arthur Conan Doyle's fictional detective, Sherlock Holmes. Other forms: Sherman, Sherwood, Woody.

Sidney: God of the Nysa. The anglicised form of the French name St Denys, kept popular since Victorian times by such entertainers as Sid Field and Sid James.

Silvester: Wood. Three popes ensured the popularity of this name in medieval Europe. It has recently been revived by the success of the actor Sylvester Stallone, hero of the 'Rocky' films.

Simon: Snub-nosed. A popular biblical name – Christ's chief disciple was called Simon Peter – that went out of fashion with the Reformation. Revived in the 1920s to become a '70s favourite. Other forms: Silas, Sim, Simeon, Simpson, Sims.

Sinclair: Shining brightly. An anglicised form of the French name St Clair, the name has been in use since last century when it was given to the writer Sinclair Lewis (1885–1951).

Spencer: Steward. The family name of the Princess of Wales was adopted as a first name in the last century and became popular this century because of the actor Spencer Tracy (1900–67).

Spike: Point, ear of corn. A newish name, promoted by the Australian humorist and writer Spike Milligan.

Stacey: Bountiful, fruitful. This short form of Eustace may also be a form of the girl's name Anastasia.

Stanhope: High stone. One of several stone names popular in the last century, but less common now.

Stanley: Stony meadow. This place name became fashionable in the late 19th century when it was given to Stanley Baldwin (1867–1947), who was twice Prime Minister and helped keep it in favour until the 1940s.

Stephen: Crown. A name made popular by two saints: the martyr who helped the Apostles spread the Gospel and the 12th-century Cistercian abbot who came from Dorset. Other forms: Etienne, Steve.

Sterling: Star. The name implying top quality was promoted this century by the acting Sterling Hayden and the racing driver Stirling Moss.

Stuart: Steward. Adopted as first names only last century, Stewart and Stuart were the family names of first the Scottish, then the English and finally the British royal families.

Terence: An anglicised form of the Irish name Turlough, it was taken by the Roman playwright-slave when he gained his freedom. Still popular today.

Theobald: Bold people. This and Tybalt are forms of the ancient name Theodbeald. The cat's names Tibby and Tabby derive from the cunning cat Tybalt in the medieval epic *Reynard the Fox*.

Theodore: Gift of God. St Theodore, Archbishop of Canterbury, is one of many saints who encouraged the name. Its recent use is due to the American President, Theodore Roosevelt (1858–1919). Other forms: Teddy, Theo, Tod.

Thomas: Twin. A favourite name since the 12th century when Thomas à Becket, the Archbishop of Canterbury, was martyred. With Richard and Henry, it makes up the nickname phrase 'Tom, Dick and Harry'. Other forms: Tamsen, Thompson, Tomas, Tommy.

Thornton: Village near thorns. This place name became a first name last century when it was given to the American playwright Thornton Wilder (1897–1975).

Timon: The hero of Shakespeare's *Timon of Athens* is a rich Athenian so generous that he becomes penniless and goes to live in a cave where he finds a pile of gold.

Timothy: Honour to God. A name taken up during the Reformation to honour St Timothy, companion of St Paul and first Bishop of Ephesus. Other form: Tim.

Titus: Sun, day. The Roman emperor Titus Flavius Vespasianus (9–79) began building the Coliseum in Rome. Gained some popularity more recently through the novels of Mervyn Peake.

Toby: God is good. This is a short form of Tobias, which was a medieval favourite. It stayed in prominence through the novelist Tobias Smollett (1721–71) and is now enjoying a revival.

Trevor: Great homestead. This form of the Welsh name Trefor was used in Wales last century, and has spread throughout Britain since the 1940s, helped by the film actor Trevor Howard who starred in the wartime film *Brief Encounter* (1945).

Tristram: Tumult, noise. The English form of the Celtic name Tristan. A name kept alive by Laurence Sterne's novel *Tristram Shandy* (1759–67) and Richard Wagner's opera about the medieval lovers Tristan and Isolde.

Troy: The name of many American towns, after the classical city, it was adopted by the American film actor Troy Donohue in the 1950s, and then crossed to Britain.

Uriah: My light is God. A biblical name, taken up during the Reformation, then made notorious by Charles Dickens' cunning villain, Uriah Heep, in *David Copperfield* (1849–50).

Vaughan: Small. This Welsh name came to Britain late last century, to be promoted by the composer Ralph Vaughan Williams (1872–1958).

Vernon: Springtime, or alder tree. Adopted as a first name early last century, it became fashionable in the 1920s.

Victor: Conqueror. Although used in medieval Britain, this name became popular through loyal Victorians, reaching its peak this century after the death of Queen Victoria.

Vincent: Victorious. The name of the most revered Spanish saint has been promoted by two Americans: the film director Vincente Minnelli and the actor Vincent Price.

Vivian: Full of life. Although more popular as a girl's name, Vivian was boosted by Benjamin Disraeli's first novel, *Vivian Grey* (1826–7).

Wallace: Celt, Welshman. A Scottish name, first used to honour the patriot William Wallace (1270–1304), that spread to the rest of Britain in the last century.

Walter: People's ruler. This Old German name was introduced by the Normans and has been popular ever since.

Warren: Folk, people. Like Walter, an Old German name, kept popular by Warren Hastings (1732–1818), first Governor General of India, and recently by the actors Warren Beatty and Warren Mitchell.

Wayne: Wagon-maker. This occupational surname became a popular first name in the US, crossing to Britain in the 1940s, where it has become a favourite.

Wilfred: Desire for peace. This ancient English name was revived when Sir Walter Scott (1771–1832) chose it for characters in both *Rob Roy* and *Rokeby*. Made popular earlier this century by the 1950s radio personality Wilfred Pickles.

William: Resolute guardian. A consistently popular name, given to four kings of England, the playwright and poet William Shakespeare (1564–1616) and chosen for the Prince of Wales's elder son William Arthur Philip Louis, born in 1982. Other forms: Bill, Billy, Gwylim, Wilem, Will, Willis, Willy.

Winston: Victorious town. This name used by the Churchill family since 1620 was given to Sir Winston Leonard Spencer Churchill (1874–1965), twice Conservative Prime Minister. Other forms: Winfield, Wingate, Winnie.

Wystan: Stony battleground. A popular name in the Midlands, after the 9th-century saint and king of Mercia. This century it was given to the poet Wystan Hugh Auden (1907–73).

Xavier: Shining. This Arabic word was given to honour St Francis Xavier (1506–52), the Spanish founder of the Jesuit order and missionary to India, Sri Lanka and Japan.

Xerxes: King. The name of the Persian king (519–465BC) who defeated the Greeks at Thermopylae.

Yule: A Norse name whose origins are either a 12-day long heathen festival or a winter month that began in mid-November.

Yves: God's mercy. The French form of the Welsh name Evan, from John.

Zak: God remembered. The shortened form of a biblical name – Zachariah was the father of John the Baptist – that was popular with the Puritans. Other forms: Zacaria, Zach, Zachery, Zeke.